AWAKENING OF THE WESTERN WOMAN

LOUISE CARRON HARRIS

LOUISE CARRON HARRIS

Cover design: Melissa Matthews

Illustration: Lizzie Owen

For my tribe

LOUISE CARRON HARRIS

CONTENTS

A woman's highest calling is to lead a man to his soul.
A man's highest calling is to protect a woman, so she is
free to walk the earth unharmed.

—Native American Proverb

Dance of the Sacred Union

We came together

Not through need to agree,

But to challenge each other

In how we see.

For you see the world

Through how you are,

And I see the world

Through my journey so far.

Your truths are yours

And mine are mine alone.

Dare we walk together

Down a road named Unknown?

You are my black

And I am your white.

You are the Yang

Grounding me from flight.

And I am your Yin

Bringing lightning and thunder.

You are my safe

As I lead us into wonder.

PREFACE

AWAKENING OF THE WESTERN WOMAN for all those whose hearts are awakening to something bigger than their mind can conceive. Despite my resistance and fear, I was divinely guided to write this book, my desire to be in service far outweighing the fear of vulnerability that comes with sharing.

This is an inward journey, one of miracles and wonder, darkness and despair, and divine union. This is my response to the sacred call of my soul's purpose, a call that is waiting for you too; if you so dare to walk the path with your shadow and be guided by your light, if you open your heart to faith and wonder, your soul will take flight.

The biggest hero in this journey is Harry, my husband. He is the representation of many men who see the world through logic and reason. He, despite my illogical and sometimes unreasonable behaviours, has opened his heart, mind and soul to the unknown.

Harry has let me share our story of the mystic, the mundane and the miracles. This book is not just about my growth, but his too. I have honoured his request to not share *everything*, but he has allowed me to share the stories that I hope will awaken something inside of you.

May these seeds of awakening be planted in your sacred garden and may an abundance of love be upon you always.

All my love,

Louise

CHAPTER 1

EVERYTHING CAN CHANGE IN A DAY

Dream life

I WAS TWENTY-FIVE years old and living the life I had always wanted. After years of always being skint and trapped in jobs that destroyed my soul, I was earning good money in a dream job that I couldn't quite believe I was doing and commuting into London every day with my soulmate.

Harry and I both felt far too young to call each other husband and wife. We were a far cry from the adulting we assumed was required to be married. In many ways, we still felt like the 17- and 19-year-olds we had been when we first met seven years earlier, a relative eternity at that age.

We were blessed, truly blessed, cocooned in love. We were each other's biggest fans. We were strong. We knew it. Everyone knew it. Our union was the epicentre of our friendship circles. We were surrounded by awesome people

— wild, fun, loyal, kind — his friends from school, my friends from university, and the new friends we met along the way from our many trips to Glastonbury Festival. We were a hub of love, laughter and adventure and I counted my blessings daily.

Harry had his feet firmly on the ground. While I was wild like the wind, Harry was the oak tree. The guys looked up to him, respected him. Every girl wanted to marry him. My girlfriends used to say, "Every girl needs a Harry," and they were right. He was a tall, dark, handsome man, kind, intelligent, logical, practical, affectionate and loyal to all things: his job, his friends and most of all me.

Harry and I were never apart, except when we were at work. Even then, we didn't like leaving each other. We would call and email each other from the moment we got into our respective offices to the moment we left. It was special and unusual. Every night before we fell asleep holding hands and just as I would slip into my dream world, I'd whisper to him, "We're so lucky, aren't we?" and he would whisper back, "We make our own luck, Lou."

I could not imagine a life without him. Harry was my soulmate, my one true love. I knew the only thing that would ever separate us was death. That meant the thought of him dying and leaving me in this world alone was my deepest fear; a fear that not so much held me captive, but more evoked a huge sense of gratitude for him and for the life we had built. It was as though some part of me knew, if I stopped being grateful, it would all end.

The awareness that death is always waiting for us, could take us in a blink of an eye, ripping us from what we love more than anything in the world, was enough temperance to soothe my sometimes fiery and dramatic nature. When arguments or tensions would rise, we would resolve them swiftly. Neither of us liked to be cross with each other for long. He was too laid back to be bothered; I was too aware that each candle had a limited burn time. The flames of life would flicker and eventually fade. The sacredness and impermanence of life was an awareness I'd had ever since I could remember. When I was a little girl, I thought I could make life last longer if I was nice to it, kind to it, as if coaxing a precious butterfly to stay one more second on the condition I revelled in its beauty and gave thanks for its presence. It was a reverence for the preciousness of life that kept Harry and I going through the rocky times and challenges of our relationship...

Never fall asleep on an argument.

Never part without a resolution.

Always say 'I love you' before leaving.

There are no guarantees that we will wake up tomorrow or see each other later.

I felt I had to keep death at bay by loving life, loving him, and being grateful for everything and everyone in my life. Every moment of life together we appreciated. We were so inseparable that even our friendship groups merged. We became the centre of a huge social circle and shared the same social life. We lived hard, partied hard, played hard and loved intensely.

Despite having moved out of the city a couple of years earlier, I loved our daily commute from the Buckinghamshire commuter belt into London town. Harry and I would jump on the train together in the morning, grab breakfast and a coffee at the train station, then jump on the Underground. We'd take the Bakerloo line to Oxford Circus together where we would part ways. Standing on that platform, we kissed passionately every morning like it was our last, oblivious to anyone watching or what people thought. And there in the stillness of the moment between the crowds dispersing and us saying goodbye, it would be just us two, every day for the last time. The rumble of the next Tube was our push to get on with the day.

"Okay, babe, time to go. Love you. Have a good day. Email me when you get in."

I would smile, taking in his dark eyes, his 6-foot-4 build and olive tanned skin. I was proud of him for many reasons. And he was fucking beautiful to look at.

"Will do. I love you infinity times two. See ya later."

Our hands parted. I would walk backwards until he slipped through the archway to the Central line. Only then would I reach for my earphones, turn up the sounds of Damian Marley, and head towards the Victoria line to work, fuelled up for the day, ready to rock my job, excited for whatever was awaiting me.

Eight hours later, I'd wonder with anticipation if he would be on the same Tube as we headed back to catch the train out to Buckinghamshire. The thought of him still made my heart flutter. I missed him so much when I was at work. We longed for the day when we could run our own business and just be together all day. Sometimes, if I could see him in another carriage on the way home, I would will him to feel my energy so he would catch my eye through the crowd. What I loved even more, though, was waiting at the train station, with my back to the barriers at the top of the escalators coming up from the Tube, and seeing if I could sense him coming. He would reach me, wrap his arms around my waist, and I would beam a huge smile. Then he would snog my face off, grab my hand, and together we would walk to catch our train home.

***

7/7

The morning of 7 July 2005 was an exciting one. I couldn't wait to get into the city. London had won the Olympic bid the night before. We had watched it all on TV, and all I wanted to do was get into town and celebrate. I knew the whole city would be out after work. It felt big. Everyone would be coming together. This was an event that was going to unite us all and I loved that feeling of unity. That knowing overwhelmed me and brought me such joy. I never paid much attention to this sort of announcement or event, but I felt like London was *my city* and I wanted to be a part of this momentous occasion.

I was an excited Labrador, smiling at anyone who caught my eye, wondering if anyone would have a random train conversation with me about the amazing Olympics news. As ever, most people were unnerved by my openness and smiles. It didn't bother me. I smiled anyway. I knew striking up random conversations with strangers on the train only came on the 23.55, when everyone was drunk and their guard was down. Only then did they ease up, realising friendly Londoners weren't either psychos or trying to crack onto them. That's when people knew it was nice to connect with strangers and have some banter.

I loved to watch the way countryside turned into city. The half-hour commute was often soundtracked by whatever tunes we had ripped off Napster and uploaded to my new ipod. I loved music. Harry did too. It was the blood in our veins. Sometimes I would choose tracks that matched the view. Sometimes tracks that evoked memories. *Hold tight, London!* I thought as the Chemical Brothers played in my ears.

As our train pulled up to the platform, Harry reached for my hand to lead me through the swarm of middle-class suits. I always stuck out. For the first time, I had money to go shopping, but with my long skirts and cowboy boots, I enjoyed looking more like an artist than a stuck-up suit. Though I liked a bit of cosmopolitan lifestyle, boho chic was in fashion, which suited my hippy spirit.

We moved down the carriage like we did every morning, his arm stretching back, his hand wrapped tightly around mine. *Always the protector, my Harry.* I was eager for those doors to open so I could weave my way through the crowds and get my hands on a copy of *Metro,* the free commuter newspaper. They were often gone by the time we got there, but I knew there would be one for me today. I had a bee in my bonnet about getting to keep a little bit of history and I couldn't wait to read it. There were a few papers left in the box and I grabbed one. In my head, I was emceeing the story of what the Olympics meant for London when the thought made my eyes fill with tears. I held my paper in my hands as though it was treasure, and stood crying with pride in Marylebone station as I took in the double page spread covered with Olympic rings. My energy levels were through the roof. Today was going to be a memorable day.

"How fucking awesome is this, babe? Tonight is going to be mental," I laughed.

"It's pretty epic," Harry replied, "Look after it. It'll be nice to keep. A little piece of history."

We each grabbed our usual bagel and coffee, and jumped on the Tube chatting about where we should all go for after-work drinks that evening.

"I'll email the gang. Maybe meet in Soho. The Argyll will be good and it will be vibing around there. I reckon everyone will just be so up for it."

"Everyone off! This Tube terminates here!" the man on the tannoy announced, interrupting my enthusiastic chatter. The usual sigh of annoyance at the disruption groaned through the train as we were made to exit the carriage. I looked at Harry.

"What's going on?"

Harry shrugged, unfazed, and reached for my hand. We began shuffling along with the rest of the crowd up to the street above. When we got outside, I pulled out my BlackBerry and called in to work to say I'd be late.

"Don't worry, Lou. There's been a power surge at Liverpool Street, so avoid going that way," Stu said casually. "Loads of disruptions everywhere. Try to jump on a bus. See you when I see you."

Sudden panic surged through me. Everyone, including Harry, seemed unbothered as though this was a mild irritation, and here I was consumed with an inner dread. Something was wrong. Very, *very* wrong. Yet I couldn't express the fear. We stood among the crowd waiting to cross the Marylebone Road to reach the buses.

Squeezing Harry's hand, I said calmly, "Babe, we need to stop and go into a cafe and listen to the news. Something feels off."

I sensed his whole body flinch with annoyance. It caught me off guard. I knew he felt the pressure of getting to work — he's an incredibly loyal, timely and organised person —

and could tell he thought I was being silly, so he ignored me coolly. I tried to reason this in my head, but the feeling that something bad was going to happen was taking over my mind. I was desperate to make him hear me.

"You need to listen to me. We can't go any further into town."

"Babe, I need to get to work," he said agitated.

We waited to cross the road and tears welled up in my eyes again. I held his hand tighter, my fear beginning to turn into anger. *Why is he being so stubborn? It'll only take 10 minutes. We're late anyway and work will understand. Everyone is going to be delayed this morning.* As we crossed the road, my rage built and built. I froze on the spot and refused to move. His huge frame looked down on me, no longer calm. His eyes filled with frustration.

"What is *wrong* with you, Lou? We need to go and get a bus."

"Babe, listen to me," I said in my softest, calmest voice, trying to get him to see I wasn't crazy. "We can't go any further into town. We need to stop and go into a cafe and listen to the news." I repeated. "Something is very wrong. It will take five minutes. Will you please trust me on this?"

We were getting in everyone's way, standing on the busy footpath arguing. Harry couldn't see where this neurotic behaviour had come from and was getting annoyed at my pestering.

"Stop it, Lou. You're being ridiculous."

The panic in my stomach jumped up into my heart. Standing in the middle of the pavement, the tension burst out of my mouth at full throttle. With equal force, he matched my anger. We were fighting for different sides, no longer a unit. We were being torn apart by anger, by ego.

"Listen to me!" I screamed again and pushed him in the chest.

I shocked myself at the forcefulness of my reaction. I saw his disgust at my dramatic behaviour and felt ashamed of myself. In the world around us, everyone was getting on with their day as though everything was normal. Just another day in London town, people running a bit late for work, trying to make their way in. But me? I was standing here having a meltdown. *Why could no-one else feel this too?*

Harry kept walking towards Marble Arch. He was walking so fast he was almost running. I would walk five steps and then freeze. Panic would rise through me and I'd say again and again, "Why won't you listen to me?"

"Grow up, Lou. You look like a dick. Sort it out."

Harry's words were awful. This was so unlike us. I begged him.

"Babe, please listen to me. Please. We can't go further into town. We need to stay here. You need to trust me that something is happening. Please, babe, listen to me. Please, Harry, please. Why can't we just wait for a while? Go and get breakfast and listen to the news or something?"

"Stop it, Lou! If you wanna go home, go. I'm going to work."

My heart was hurting. I felt trapped. That wasn't the answer I wanted. I looked down at the ground trying to work out what was going on in my mind. I was so confused at the energy between us, the energy around us, the energy within me.

"Pull yourself together or go and get the train back home," he snapped.

I looked at him tears rolling down my face.

"I need to get to work, Lou," he sighed, "Either get on the bus with me now or go home. The station is just there."

All I knew is that we needed to get away from the city, but I wouldn't go without him. Even though he couldn't see it, this was the moment I had always feared. I would rather die next to him than have him die and leave me here in this world on my own. I was aware of the strong dramatic feelings that were surfacing. I questioned if I *really was* losing the plot and delving into some fantasy. Then the adrenaline rushing around my body pushed me further out and I began to observe the situation from an almost elevated place.

"Please don't leave me, babe. Please listen to me. I don't want to argue. You know I don't want to argue, but I just need you to listen to me. I just need to listen to the news," I sobbed.

My pathetic behaviour triggered him. He was more pissed off than I'd ever seen him. I had pushed him in the past, but he was different this time and it frightened me. And yet, he was looking for any way to defuse the situation. Everyone was looking at us and he was embarrassed. He hated being seen like this, being the focus of drama. He always cared what people thought more than I did.

"FINE! We'll get the bus to my office and you can come in and listen to whatever you need to listen to there, but I need to get to work. You can either come with me now or go back home. Either way, I am leaving right *now*."

I had to go with him. I'd never seen it this busy before. There were so many people around. We somehow managed to climb onto the back of a Routemaster bus heading towards Holborn. We squeezed in at the back and I leaned my head on the handrail. For a few moments, I tried to calm myself from the terror in my heart. I felt the breeze coming through the doors, cooling my burning cheeks.

"There's one seat upstairs at the back, love," the conductor said to me, sympathetically.

"I'm okay here, thanks," I said trying not to sob harder at the kindness of his voice.

I looked at the back of Harry's head, so desperately wanting to connect with him. He moved to let someone else on the bus. I tried to catch his gaze, but he was detached, his eyes transfixed on the window. My heartbeat was racing. Everything was so wrong. His unusual coldness hurt as much as the fear that we were going somewhere we shouldn't.

There was a sense of urgency within me. Tremors of fear, sadness, anger and confusion rolled up and down my body. Waves of anxiety crashed on my soul, drowning and choking me. I could still feel his anger and now I was angry. It was a brick wall preventing us from looking at each other. I understood why he was baffled by my reactions. Even I was! But my intuition was so strong that I was furious he hadn't taken me seriously. *Why won't he listen to me? He is risking our lives for his work instead of trusting me.*

I had my eyes fixed on the door and the world outside. I could feel the hustle and bustle of London life going on as normal. On any other day, I loved to ride on the bus. I was a people-watcher. I enjoyed the diversity when the overspill of corporate media types fought their way through the tourists on Oxford Street. But today I did *not* love it. Today I did *not* want to be here.

As the bus pulled up at the first stop, I caught eyes with a guy getting on. He squeezed through looking worn down and fed up. There was something about him that made me desperately sad. *Does he know, too? If he does, why is he going further?* I wondered.

Everyone else looked composed and regular, but he looked like I felt. My body reacted to his disposition. I started sweating, my body burning, my blood rushing, pulsing in my head as if it was going to explode. Everything around me was bright and light. I felt sick. Static in my brain buzzed as loudly as a gale. *Something really isn't right. How can the world around be so still and calm when I'm physically combusting?*

When the bus began to pull away, something took me over. I didn't know what I was doing. I was removed from my body. But for some reason, I was jumping off. I stumbled onto the pavement, confused at my impulse. I looked behind me, back at the bus, and there was Harry at the door.

"Harry, get off now!"

He jumped out of responsibility, with fury in his eyes. I didn't even recognise him. And I didn't even care.

"What the *fuck*, Lou? For fuck's sake, what were you thinking!? All the buses are full and now we'll have to walk the rest of the way! For *fuck's* sake!"

For some reason, I didn't argue with him for the rest of the walk to his work. He was shouting at me, but he was shouting at a shell. I had popped out of my body to safety. I was floating somewhere behind us as we made our way past Oxford Circus towards his offices in Holborn. There was a relief inside me. I had a plan. I was going to get to his office, watch the news. I was going to be safe, safe from this idea I'd probably made up in my head! I tried to make conversation with Harry, but it was in vain. I tried to hold Harry's hand, but he shrugged me away. I had pushed him to his limits, behaved badly, 'irrationally.' Now we had to walk another half an hour and it was my fault he'd be so late for work.

I calmed myself. The sense of peace was easier to tune in to now we were out in the open. I felt less trapped and safer knowing we would get to his office and be away from whatever it was that was crippling my rationality. Barely a word passed between us in half an hour and I knew he was only able to think about how he'd let down his team by not being there. There was no connection between us. The walk was painful, but I was only grateful to feel safe again.

We reached the large swing doors. As we went to walk in, Harry turned to me and said, "Right, I've gotta go. I'll see you later. Let me know when you get into work."

His voice was cold and factual. He didn't even go to kiss me goodbye. My mind raced. He'd said I could come to his office. He'd said I could come *in*. My workplace was a half-hour Tube ride from Holborn, where we were now. The only way there was via Liverpool Street, but I knew I shouldn't go there. I just knew.

"How am I going to get to work? You said I could come in."

"Get the Tube, Lou. It's late. I need to work."

"Fuck you, Harry, fuck you!" I screamed at him, as he made his way through the doors. "I'll have to go to Liverpool Street from here!"

I'd been hoping he would see that was a bad idea and stop me going, but he walked on.

"Fuck you! I can't actually believe you're letting me go! Fuck you. Fuck *you*."

I spun on my heels and stormed off in a fit of rage, no doubt leaving Harry relieved that he was at work, finally away from the insanity of the past hour and a half. We had never in seven years parted ways like this. And now, at a time when I felt I was looking into a hole of despair, where all I could feel was death, we were parting in a way that went against every belief system etched into my soul. Our bond had broken. We were broken. I was walking to Liverpool Street alone. It felt like walking towards the storm without anyone by my side. I stopped caring. I stopped crying. I went numb. And the inexplicable intuition continued in me.

I tried reasoning with myself as I walked. Harry was safe. That's all that mattered. I could die and it wouldn't matter because at least I wouldn't be left alone on this earth without him. I didn't care what happened now. As I walked, these thoughts turned over in my mind. Yet I just couldn't understand how he could do this to me; leave me to walk away like this.

Somewhere along High Holborn, the same intense feeling that took over when I jumped from the bus told me to look up. A bus passed with a 'Not In Service' sign on it. Then another. And another. Then everywhere I looked streams of buses with the same 'Not In Service' sign came down the street. The blood drained from me. I looked around at people. Everyone was still. No-one was walking. It was eerie, a time lapse. Hundreds of people all just stopped, staring at their mobiles. The darkest of all fear was now over us. We all felt it, unaware of *why*. I pulled out my phone. There was no reception. Nothing. I could feel that something terrible had happened. My body ached.

In a split second, people were moving again, hurriedly, in flight. The next thing I knew I was running, running back to Harry's office. I had to be with Harry. There were crowds of people going the opposite way to me, but I was trying desperately to get back to the one person that mattered in all this mayhem.

And then, there he was, running towards me, hand outstretched through the crowd. He reached, grabbed my shoulder and dragged me back through the people. I was crying, though I don't remember when I'd started again.

"I'm sorry. I'm so sorry. You were right."

Harry looked so frightened.

"A bomb went off on a bus just behind the office. It *shook*. Lou, we have to get back to my office. It's bombproof and it's going into lockdown. We have to get there and *stay* there."

Harry was pulling me to safety. We reached his office and went up to his floor. Everyone was gathered around the TV. I sat down with them in shock and watched in horror as the news programmes began to report what had happened to our city that morning.

At 8.49am, three Tube trains had been blown up in succession: one at Aldgate, one at Edgware Road, one at Russell Square. At 9am, the number 30 bus was diverted from Marble Arch to Baker Street to collect the thousands of passengers who could not get on Tubes. At 9.47, the bus was blown up outside Tavistock Square.

"I told you. I told you, Harry! Why didn't you listen to me? That could have been us!" I cried.

He closed down on me, responding with a cold, sharp, "It's just a coincidence, Lou. Stop being so dramatic."

I was furious at him, but deeply fearful that what was happening in our city was a reflection of what was happening in our relationship. Dutifully, Harry went to his desk and carried on working. I wandered aimlessly around the office. I wasn't allowed to leave during the lockdown, but suddenly I felt like I was in his space, trespassing in his world. So I sat in the loo, crying in disbelief that this could ever happen in this city, trying to understand my intuitions of the morning, and wrapping my head around the reality that people had died today.

I spent the rest of the morning checking emails on my BlackBerry, watching news reports on TV, and drinking coffee. One by one, our gang of friends checked in with each other, and by 11am, I knew everyone I loved was safe. At 3.30pm, we got news that we were allowed to leave the building. Harry and I still hadn't spoken about what had happened, but he came and found me, told me to go home and that he'd see me later.

"But you finish in an hour. I may as well wait."

"Just go home, Lou," Harry repeated, "I'll see you later."

As we kissed goodbye, there was a sense of distance between us. I called Harry's best friend Mark as I walked back along the same route we'd taken that morning, too frightened to get on a Tube. I cried through fear of what was happening between me and Harry, fear that something had broken between us, and fear of the way I had to go home. Mark soothed me on the phone for 45 minutes, making me feel safe as I walked those streets again, comforting me about Harry.

"Lou, you know he'll be feeling guilty. Don't push him. You're Harry and Lou. You'll get through this, because the world wouldn't spin without you two."

***

CHAPTER 2

CERTAIN THERE'S 'SOMETHING'

Pull of presence

IT'S POSSIBLE FOR US to yearn for something we don't even know exists, to seek a feeling we have never experienced, to have a sense of 'knowing' deep inside that there is something more. Something we can't see, feel or describe, but we know is there, just waiting for us to find it. Those of us who wander this earth seeking that 'something' have a seed of aliveness inside us, a sense of hope, faith, wonder, like a tiny light breaking through the darkness.

Many laugh at our foolish desires and dreams, confused by the restlessness that arises from our beings, and urge us to get back to 'the real world', a world where their own hope has been replaced by heaviness and doubt.

We have a short moment in time where we have a choice of which path we follow. And you know, there is always that choice: to 'get real' in someone else's version of reality or to follow the threads of wonder into the unknown of your own, a reality where there is infinite possibility, where true love and magic really do exist.

***

It was deep connection I was seeking — although I didn't fully understand the yearning at six years old — when I would cry at those 80s adverts of the people standing on mountaintops holding hands and singing. I wanted to be a part of something like that. I wanted to make that happen in my world. I began to find myself lying awake night after night, watching the moon and my favourite star constellation pass by my window.

How can l get every single person in the world to stop what they're doing for one minute and hold hands with the person next to them? I thought as I lay in my bed, wide awake but heavy with responsibility. I would visualise a human chain, people coming out of their houses one by one to reach for the strangers next to them. I imagined streams of love passing through their hands. I could feel what it would be like: their eyes would light up, smiles on their faces as they connected with these strangers like old friends. I could see their hearts filling with so much love. And in that one minute, the whole world would feel peaceful, happy, connected. And everything would be good again.

The idealism of a united world followed me around. Even as a child, my mind could not resist going there, making this happen. A problem needed to be solved! I was a magnet attracting more and more ideas, more and more plans, more and more problems. I would lie there listening to music on my ever-present Walkman; music soundtracking my idealism, my worries, my responsibilities. When I learned that the consequence of lying awake all night was feeling awful in the morning, I would try to will my incessant mind to stop thinking. *I have to stop by the time my clock radio clicks over to 22:22.*

Sometimes it worked. Other times, the thoughts just went on and on and on.

What about the wars? my mind would ask me.

Oh no, I hadn't thought about that, another voice replied.

I'll just find all the names of all the men who run all the wars and write them a really nice letter asking them if they wouldn't mind stopping the war for one minute while everyone links up and holds hands, my mind would reason.

What about people driving on the motorways? What about the time zones? It will be night time in America and everyone will be in bed, the voice again.

It was exhausting carrying the weight of the world, but a nice distraction from the real wars waging at home. The older I got, the more impossible the task seemed. It became as unlikely for me to unite 5 billion people in holding hands as it was to unite my parents in amiability through their messy divorce.

As with most empath kids who feel they're from another planet to most people, I could feel every damn thing everyone in my life was feeling. I could read every intention of adults — teachers, strangers, my parents of course. The energetic war between them was painful to me in many ways. I was sensitive to their emotions. I took their short fuses personally. I formed my world view when my own world was falling apart, devising clever strategies to keep the peace... *Be as nice and as useful as possible. Don't ask for anything. Never be a burden. Then people will want me.* Communication doesn't need to be verbal. I knew that much was true, since I'd watched my parents say a thousand things and not even open their mouths. I could feel the constant transmission of their thoughts and emotions, like watching a game of attack and defence over a power neither of them ever felt they had. I nominated myself to try to make everyone feel better by saying kind words and delivering compliments with a smile. I could see the invisible cords between them, transmitting the energy of their wounds and hurts. Even though my dad lived 10 miles away, I knew words and thoughts were sent down those cords between them and received like invisible messages, in pangs of fear, anxiety, vulnerability, sadness, anger. I saw all humans did this to each other. They just didn't realise what they were doing.

***

Up in the stars

At seven years old, a teacher showed me how to find three stars in a line not far from the moon — Orion's Belt. If I carried on looking up a little further, I would find a cluster called The Seven Sisters. Every night I would search for those stars, proud of myself for finding it on my own. I became smitten, climbing out of bed, sometimes opening my window to see if I could see those seven beautiful sisters. They twinkled at me, brought me peace, as if that was really my home. *If only I could fly there.*

I had a feeling there was more out there than I could see. If I stared at the moon, I was sure something would happen. If I talked to a tree, I thought maybe it would talk back. *Keep looking, Lou,* something would tell me. But nothing happened. Nothing ever did. And I was even beginning to lose my faith in fairies...

It was to be another 30 years before I would learn how important these stars were, not just for me and for many other sensitive children who felt like they were not from this world, but for every ancient culture on the earth, from Native Americans to Aboriginal people, Mayans, Greeks and Egyptians, who were all awake to the 'something' more...

***

School was hard. I couldn't learn anything. I was dyslexic. I could read people, not books. I was socially intelligent but academically stuck. I thought I was thick and incapable of learning, so that story played out through my education. I never understood that I simply learned in ways that didn't fit the mould. I found freedom in learning how to become invisible if I needed. Other times, I would charm teachers away from asking me humiliating questions that I couldn't answer.

I used to slip out of the school gates at lunchtime to escape the uncomfortable void of not belonging and lose myself in music. I'd listen to Michael Jackson, releasing the heaviness on my heart of wishing everyone would be happy. I would climb to the top of the tallest slide on an old deserted concrete playground, light up a Silk Cut cigarette stolen from my mum's stash and take a moment, allowing the music to immerse me. I'd stand with my arms open, tears streaming down my face, feeling every word of *Heal The World* pulling on my heartstrings. I would feel my desire to bring people together in love, faith, hope and deep peace.

There were human angels all around me in my life. I moved schools and fell into the loving arms of nine amazing girls who accepted me for me. We were never bothered by the popular crowds. We were all a little alternative and quirky and kind.

The head of year pulled me aside within the first month of my new school.

"Lou, you and I both know you've been put into sets that are too high for your ability, but we have no records from your last school. I know you're not able to cope with the work in this set, but I've thought about it and sense dropping you down isn't going to help. I can see the bonds you've formed with your new friends, and that will be more important for you, so I'm going to make you a deal. I will bypass this if you promise to come tell me when you need help and do your best to stay ahead."

And so I practised hiding my inability to learn, read or retain information. My best friends let me copy their homework and helped me when I was sinking.

The summer of GCSEs came along, but no matter how much I tried, I couldn't revise or remember anything. I couldn't even understand it. I would wake up every morning, clean my room, get myself a coffee and sit down with the intention of really getting *something* into my head. But no. I realised everyone else had a revision plan. And I didn't. I cried. I was lost, panicked. *What happens if I fail everything?*

I sat in the front garden, sun shining, and loaded my Walkman with some new batteries and a cassette that had come free on the front of the latest *NME* music newspaper. As the tape played, I lit a cigarette and laid back in the soft grass, gripped by a new song. Something strange started happening. My entire body felt weird, like a power source was coming through me. *Am I dying?* Then my body began to vibrate, my heart began to expand, an energy rose through me like a light pulling me up, yet I felt like my body was pinned to the ground. *Something* was happening to me. It was as if I was watching myself in a movie. Physically, it was unlike anything I'd felt before. Almost like... euphoria!

Tears flowed down my cheeks as the energy washed through me. The world around seemed so bright and everything inside was tingling. It wasn't like getting high or drinking vodka. It was unreal, but peaceful. *Something* was with me. An angel perhaps? And in that moment, I knew. I knew my exams didn't matter, everything was going to be alright. More than alright.

The last of the lyrics rang in my head, 'Fly on, my sweet angel', and as the music stopped, I came out of my trance. Disorientated, I tried to make sense of it all. I tried getting back to it, trying to retrace my steps to make it happen again. I wanted to feel that feeling, that peace and safety.

Over that summer, I found glimmers of that same energy. I could taste it if I relaxed in a hot bath, or put on some relaxing music. Sometimes an old tape with Peruvian panpipes would transport me to the Andes. I could almost feel myself in those mountains, touching the same sort of peace, but never quite got that angel to visit me again with her electric magic.

***

Necessary path of self-destruction

I tasted love at sweet 16. A boy swept me off my feet in the sixth form at high school. He was a romantic soul who would shake the blossom from the tree as I danced under the falling petals on our walks home. We would write poems and love letters to each other every day. Within weeks, we began to explore each other's minds, bodies and souls. He led me to a place of deep connection. He led me to the sacred waters of my own divine feminine power. He taught me about my own pleasure, mutual pleasure and the sacredness of making love. We broke up when I went away to begin a new life at university, but he had created a standard of expectation within me that was — from then on — hard to meet.

For a while, I sat in lectures in my Music Management degree at university with a blank face. Then, to avoid the painful truth that I had no idea what they were talking about, I stopped going altogether. I distracted myself from my academic struggles by going out and pulling boys who could, for some small amount of time, make me feel worthy.

One wet Sunday in early 1998, I sat in the dark with shame rolling round my body. I had come back to university after Christmas and straight away poisoned myself with too much vodka and too many cigarettes. My throat hurt. I felt shit.

A memory of the night before sent my body cringing, my mind churning out a million fears. I plunged my head into the pillow attempting to erase the memories of the outrageous things I had said and done in the last few months, but especially the sickening feeling from the night before. Mainly the shame of how I had fallen into my room with one of the rugby boys at the end of the night. We'd stripped off. He'd pushed me onto the bed, got on top of me, all over me. He hadn't been kind, hadn't kissed me in the loving way I knew I deserved, more grabbing and groping until his naked body was on top of mine and I positioned myself to do what was expected...

"What are you *doing*?" he'd said, pulling back and laughing at me.

I'd looked at him confused, ashamed that I'd done something wrong, though I didn't know what.

"I've got a girlfriend," he'd mentioned then, as though I should have known, as though it was the most normal thing in the world to be half-fucking another girl. He'd looked at me disgusted.

"I can't *actually* have sex with you! Can't you just go down on me?"

I had jumped off the bed, grabbed a towel and screamed at him to get out. He had followed me into the kitchen, wrapping himself in a towel too.

"Lou, come on, don't be like that. Let's go back," he'd coaxed.

"*No!* Fuck off. Get out of my flat."

That's when he'd walked up to me and started kissing my neck.

"Sorry Lou, come on. Let's go back."

I remembered wanting desperately for him not to reject me. Attempting to rid myself of the shame in an already awful situation, I'd agreed. Back in the bedroom, he'd grabbed my waist, pulled off the towel and kissed me. Fully naked, he'd laid me on the bed, parted my legs and slotted in-between me. He'd kissed me again, as I'd begun to move into him.

"What the fuck, Lou?" he'd shouted in my face, "I *told* you I can't have sex with you. I have a girlfriend!"

More shame, masked by rage, masked by confusion, had overtaken my entire my body and I'd pushed him off me, screamed at him at the top of my lungs.

"Get the fucking *fuck* out of my life. Get the fuck out. Get the fuck out."

He'd pushed me against the door, trying to hug me, to kiss me, to calm me down.

"Shhh, come on, Lou. Don't be like this. We can do other things," he'd tried kissing me but I hadn't wanted to kiss him. I'd wanted him out, wanted to cry, but not in front of him.

"Please, just get out," I'd sighed.

Then he'd reached my hand above my head, pinned me to the door and stroked my face. He'd looked me in the eye giving me the sense that he almost pitied me. Then, leaning in as if to kiss my neck, he'd whispered, "Can you just finish me off, Lou?"

Looking at him in disgust, I'd grabbed my towel and left my own room, charged down the hallway and locked myself in the shower room. I had turned the water on as hot as it would go and stood on the cold tiles sobbing, willing him to be gone by the time I got back. I'd wanted to escape myself, to do something, anything, just to get away from the torture going on inside me, that familiar sense of shame flooding the vacant space in my body. I had mind-fucked myself into oblivion, every thought self-chastising, my mind on overdrive, thinking back to all I had done in the past six months or so, thoughts of self-loathing and disgust.

So there I was the next morning, ashamed and sad, taking my hungover body off the student campus to the cinema where I sobbed uncontrollably throughout *Titanic* for the second time in a week.

On returning to the halls of residence that Sunday evening, I closed the door of my bedroom and broke into a shaking, pissed off, emotional wreck. No more did I want to be available to everyone, to be the centre of attention. I was ready to do something I rarely did: be alone with myself. My door was now closed, my curtains pulled tight. I searched through a pile of CDs with bleary eyes, trying to find something as soothing as the music in the movie. I had nothing in my drum and bass collection. I sifted through a pile I had borrowed from various other students on campus and came across some classical, lent to me by a flatmate who'd probably hoped to make me less noisy to live with.

I dug out a candle I'd been given for Christmas and filled my room with the scent of orange. I lay back on my bed and watched the way the flame's reflections danced across the back of my door. As I looked around, I realised I rarely saw my room this way. In this light, the room was a cocoon, a womb. I began to surrender the black shadow living in my body. I sat in the pain. There was nowhere to escape. I felt sorry for myself and all I could do was sob.

A loneliness and desperation for someone I'd never even met entered me. I felt a sudden longing for a person who would discover the hidden mysteries and depth of what was possible inside of me, inside of them. I wanted to sink deep into their soul and merge into one. It was in this state that I had it out with God, not that I believed in one at the time, but I found myself on my knees, sobbing out my pain, giving it all up to a God I didn't even know.

I've had enough. I can't be alone anymore. My heart is breaking. I don't want to fuck and run. I don't want to wait any longer. I'm so fucking lonely. Where is my love? Where is the guy who will love me unconditionally, the One who will last forever? Send him to me. I gazed at the photos of my friends, my family, my home town. I felt so alone, yet I didn't want any of them. I wanted this other someone. Through the sobs, I found a way to release this pain inside me. I grabbed a blue biro from my desk, tore a page from my notepad and began to draw. In some ways, I was embarrassed, as though someone invisible may be watching and judging me on my ability to draw nothing more than a stick man, but I was compelled to continue. There came a boat on the sea, dark clouds, a moon.

I observed myself, tears and snot dripping on the paper, shouting at a God unknown to me, commanding that I have true love, a real deep love. I wanted a guy who would love me unconditionally, who I could love unconditionally. I wanted true love. I watched the way I coloured over and over the lines, filling in the gaps of the sea, careful not to go through the paper. I moved beyond the judgment of my imperfections. This was for me now, and only for me. I felt my sadness, my emptiness, pouring out of me through the pen. As I wiped my tears with the back of my hand, I lost grip of the pen and let it slip on the page, but I was so intently focused, nothing mattered. None of this had to be perfect. I wanted to keep doing this forever. It was as if something other than me was drawing.

Whatever it was, it felt good. The pen moved the sadness and desperation out of my body. The more I drew over and over the lines, the more powerful I felt. Something was happening to me. I was almost floating. I sensed that I'd felt something like this before in my life but I couldn't pinpoint it. By the time I finished, I felt a release. Almost like... *euphoria.*

I lit a cigarette and sat in the overwhelm, watching myself as though I was watching a movie. It was a beautiful feeling, and a memory that stayed with me for years.

I tore off another sheet of paper and began to write. Words came out of my pen before my mind could even think them. I wrote and wrote and wrote, some sense, some nonsense, random words, half-sentences, feelings. I had no idea what I was writing. I had never written anything outside of school, other than a love letter to my first boyfriend, but this was different. This was healing me. This was well beyond my norm. I had no idea who was writing, who I was writing to, what I was writing for. The words came from my soul — begging, pleading, asking, asking something, asking someone, to come and help me, to release me from my shame, to heal my pain, to send me the love I had longed for all my life.

I passed out that night not from lager or vodka, as I normally would, but from a total release of the emotional weight I had been carrying around for what felt like a lifetime.

The next morning, I woke up with a sense of liberation. Somehow, I had made it through the birth canal to an upgraded version of my true self — lighter and brighter! I was exhausted but excited for what felt like a new life waiting for me. I made myself a coffee in the kitchen, taking care to avoid my flatmates, trying to keep the sacredness I felt all around me. Back in my bedroom, I put on a CD, opened my window and felt the cool morning air on my skin. I sat cross-legged looking at what I'd drawn the night before and at the random words on the page. None of this made much sense, but it didn't have to. I held on to this new feeling, in awe of what had happened. It was as though I had cleared something inside me that I didn't know needed clearing. I had connected deeper into my own soul, swum in my own ocean, gone so deep that I'd found a dark heavy chest on the ocean floor and released all that was trapped inside. The crappy drawing could have been mistaken for one made by a small child, but it didn't matter. Something magical had happened. I had no idea what, but I knew it was good. I had honoured my soul, connected to her and loved her enough to spend some time listening. I had been a best friend to myself when I needed one. I felt this strange love and nurtured it in my womb.

I felt fucking amazing.

Thereafter, I moved with the seasons, hibernating for the rest of the winter, hanging out with friends, happy to go home to an empty bed on a Friday night. I was more grounded. I went into that spring a little different to how I was before. I had some kind of self-love that I'd not had for a while. There were fewer boys in my bed, but more late nights with good friends and laughter. And in this space, the more I witnessed my self-respect and confidence, the more decent people gravitated towards me.

It was like my scrawled pleas had been sent to my angels and they had answered my prayers.

***

Twin flames

He was so beautiful — tall, dark, handsome, beautiful brown eyes, the gentlest energy, clearly popular, surrounded by friends. He was casually confident the way he smoked his cigarette, chatting to his gang of friends, but shy when he came to the bar to order a pint.

I had begun to notice him at the start of the summer holidays, having decided to stay in my university town rather than go home. I was working in the coolest pub in town. The bar was like a stage for us bartenders — water fights, flirting and dancing alongside serving pints! Yet I was convinced he had hardly noticed me.

Then again, I *knew* so deeply that this guy was my guy, my One. Over time, our eyes would meet, but he was too shy to approach me and I was too scared of rejection from someone out of my league. Then strange 'coincidences' began to happen that made me pay attention. Every time he walked into the pub, the jukebox would play the same song: *What Can I Do To Make You Love Me?* It happened every shift for a week, and then the next week, and the next. *How does that even happen?* It was so weird, even my manager began to notice it.

"It's like some sort of weird magic love spell, you crazy witch!" my manager would joke.

What could I do to make him love me? And stop this yearning for him?

***

I was feeling something in my bones. It was Saturday night of the August bank holiday weekend and I had the night off. Dressed up in my best black top, shortest skirt and knee-high boots, I marched behind the bar to help myself to a drink. There he was waiting to be served. I took a deep breath, leaned over the bar and dared to speak to him.

"Coming to Club Eden later?"

"Yeah, I am. I'll see you there?" he smiled, then wandered off back to his mates.

Oh my God, he spoke to me.

"Good for you, Lou. Don't do anything I wouldn't!" my manager laughed.

A few hours later, I opened the door of my new student house and showed Harry into my room. We had snogged the second I'd walked into the club but it was too noisy to talk in there. I'd suggested we go to mine, a short walk away, but his friends were expecting him back. He'd assumed he was just walking me home.

"I'll be back in a second. I'm just going to the bathroom. Make yourself comfortable," I said with confidence. He mumbled a few shy words, seeming out of his depth, and clearly unaware of my intentions as I headed off to the shower, half wondering what the fuck I was doing and half on autopilot.

I stood in the shower thinking, *I shouldn't do this, I might actually be in love with him. How can I be in love with him? I've never even had a full conversation with him.*

He was perched on the edge of my bed looking like he was about to leave, when he saw me re-enter the room, now in just a small pink towel. His eyes widened and his energy shifted. He realised... As we kissed long and deep, his naivety transformed. He became the man I had seen him to be from afar all these weeks. His hands pressed firmly on my back as I unbuttoned his shirt to feel his skin on mine. As I felt his strong body on top of me, I was home. *It's you. I know it's you.*

I knew he was the one I had asked for in that note to the heavens. I was eager to go further and connect deeper, but overconfidence transformed into vulnerability. I was overwhelmed, as his soul entered mine. It was like a key in a lock, like stepping through a new threshold into a place I had never been before. Yet I knew him. I really knew him. It felt familiar, real.

We moved together, danced a new dance like we had danced it a million times before, our bodies getting to know each other, but our souls remembering. I moved on top of him confidently, like a powerful goddess, drinking in the way he looked at me in awe and wonder, as if all of this was as unbelievable to him as it was to me. Our eyes were locked and we came together in the way old souls do when they reconnect. *Finally, I've found you.*

I woke in his arms. He was quiet, shy, but comfortable with me. We lay together, not talking about anything much, just kissing and being close. I ignored the thoughts trying to cloud my mind, *You've ruined this already. You never sleep with your 'forever man' on the first night. You should have saved yourself.*

There was never any question in his mind. There were no games, no dramas. Apart from once three weeks later, when he admitted he wasn't in fact 23, but 17 and still at school! It didn't matter. He loved me and we were together. It was that simple. I didn't want to be apart from him and he didn't want to be apart from me. We were sociable, though, always in the centre of a crowd. Like a magnetic force, people just wanted to be with us. 'Harry and Lou' became a thing. We were solid as rock, safe and secure for each other, and for other people too.

Barely six months into our relationship, he asked me to marry him, although he wasn't proposing per se. It was more a sweeping statement one Tuesday afternoon while we were in bed together; where we were spending a considerable amount of our time! My head on his chest, my fingers running down the line of hair, he said casually, "One day, when we get married..." I can't even remember what he went on to say. The sentence seemed to stop time and I fell into a trance, processing the certainty in his voice. Though I already knew he was my soulmate and that one day we *would* get married, there was a sudden reality that this was actually him; this *was* my forever man, the one I had commanded from the God I didn't quite believe in only a year before.

In waves of blissful security, I smiled into myself, pressing my face closer into his body. *Of course we would get married one day.* I had been blessed with a knowing that he only saw in one direction. And that was me.

"So, you think we're going to get married then, knobber?" I joked.

His huge brown eyes looked down at me. Even at 17, he had a magnetic energy, powerful yet innocent.

"Of course I do, babe," he said, matter of fact.

He loved me so deeply. There was no denying that. The rivers of our connection ran deep, but I had never thought about *actual* marriage before. I don't suppose he had *thought* about it much either until that moment, yet these words fell out of his mouth so naturally, without drama, dialogue or preconception. It was all just so simple; the flow of it natural. It was as though my will, his will and God's will aligned, and a path was laid for me to walk. So I walked it.

"I love you," he said, pulling me back on top of him.

"I love you more."

"Well, I love you infinity."

"Well, I love you infinity times two."

He laughed at this.

"You can't times infinity; that's the point!"

"I can do what I like. What I say goes! I love you infinity times two."

And I meant it.

***

CHAPTER 3

ALL ROADS LEAD TO THE RIGHT PEOPLE AND PLACES

Family

THERE WAS NO GRAND gesture that Boxing Day morning in 1999 when he gave me the ring. It was straightforward for us both. A few weeks earlier, we'd played 'let's pretend to be grown-ups' and gone looking at the millennium diamonds in a jewellery shop. We didn't have any money. We spent it all on going out. But then Harry said, "Why don't we just get one and pay it off monthly?" and we went from there. The next moment, it's the day after Christmas and he's handing me a box and I'm putting a diamond on my finger as casually as any other day.

If it wasn't for my auntie, who caught him giving it to me quietly in the doorway of my mum's kitchen, we may have gotten away with it not being a big deal. As it turned out, she squealed, "Oh my God, it's going on *that* finger. Oh my God!" Mum looked up from the oven with a confused and surprised, yet warm look on her face. Then suddenly, all this unexpected attention came our way. I suppose we hadn't thought about it too much, but from then on, this engagement thing got real!

I watched my mum and stepdad, grandparents, aunts, uncles, great aunts, great uncles, parents' friends, grandparents' friends, and all the cousins, dancing, singing, drinking and laughing in the party room of the beautiful home my parents had created over the years. Beyond the gorgeous décor and two Christmas trees, this room was overflowing with genuine love. *We're a family that just love people*, I thought to myself. *We just all love each other.* I wanted to be like my mum and stepdad, who opened their doors and hearts to everyone who came into their lives, no airs and graces, no ego, just love and joy. My stepdad adored my mum and would do his best to make her happy. They were a good team too, even running a business together. My stepdad had walked into my life when I was six and taught me what sort of man I deserved. Harry was just that — kind, fun, tactile, loving.

I reflected with gratitude on how my mum had a vision and would make it happen, and how my stepdad would never let negative beliefs enter his world. He seemed able to make the impossible possible with his joyful attitude. And when she had an idea, she would nurture it, and take pride and care in everything, an attribute I seemed to lack.

"You're too easy-come easy-go, Lou," she would tell me.

No matter what I did, I couldn't seem to come out looking as neat and polished as they did, and my then-student home was a dump. Nevertheless, I hoped to have a place one day where I could hold parties, where everyone felt free, happy, affectionate, playful.

I pulled up a bar stool and joined my family, Harry smoking at the bar, us younger members of the family drinking with the older generations. They were mischief too in their day, according to my uncles, who told us stories of the crazy antics they got up to in the late 60s. And we all laughed as my stepdad told his ancient jokes.

Love and laughter radiated from this home. I wished that one day I would have a place where friends and family would gather and celebrate life.

***

Birth of a new millennium

DISSERTATIONS WERE HANDED in and our student house was the hub of all mayhem. It was the year 2000, a summer of love, a new millennium and one long ride of house parties, sunrises, and friends old and new. Our student digs were the polar opposite to the tidy house I'd grown up in. We were filthy. The sofa contained things that bit you. The shower contained things that crawled around. It was damp. It stank. And it was awesome. Because it was the best party house in town.

"Do the lights, Harry. Do the lights!" we would shout over the music. He would stand by the door as my girlfriends and I danced on the bed and desk to his makeshift strobe, in time to the beats from Harry's impressive sound system. We would laugh and laugh, and hug each other, and dance some more, drinking, drinking, drinking until the sun began to shine. Then we would all lie on the bed together, stroking each other's hair, saying, "I love you. I fucking love you. No, really, I fucking love you, man."

There was always a core of people, then strangers who would turn up and entertain us no end. There were no boundaries or borders for those with clean intentions. Everyone was invited, weekend after weekend, until the end of the summer.

Harry was the anchor for our gang and I was the mother hen, ensuring everyone had everything they needed. When the 4am chill came, I would hand out Harry's clothes, and the girls who'd turned up in little dresses and heels would parade around in his socks, jumpers, sometimes even boxer shorts. No-one cared. There was no judgment in this house. And while I hadn't quite got the house my parents had, I'd created a hub of fun for a season.

The fun went on and on that summer. Then we broke into Glastonbury Festival and it changed my whole world.

"You don't need a ticket. The fence is down. Me and the guys are gonna break in this evening. Get your shit together. We're leaving in a couple of hours."

My heart was rushing. I'd never broken into anything before. I was naughty in the way skiving off lectures and partying like a lunatic was naughty, but breaking into a festival seemed a stretch too naughty for me. And yet my body was screaming, *YES! YES! YES!*

Before I knew it, Harry and I were in Argos grabbing a cheap two-man tent and sleeping bags, and loading a box of beer and three of my girlfriends into my battered red Vauxhall Nova. No-one had any concept of what we were getting ourselves into. We also weren't aware that hundreds of thousands of people had been given the heads-up too! It was the first summer when everyone had a phone, the first summer of text messages, and the news spread like wildfire.

And I wasn't prepared for how much this experience was going to blow my mind and shift my soul.

I don't remember much of what happened that weekend. We walked around in a daze of awe, feeling like we'd travelled to a new planet. Between you and me, there were over half a million people there that year, 400,000 more than should have been there. It was near-impossible to move anywhere and there were no toilets. It was dirty, hot and edgy. It was extremes. It was survival and revival. Just by being there, I began to feel *that* feeling; the one I'd felt on my front lawn at 15 years old. There was something about this place...

Yet I had no idea it was going to be the night of my first energetic awakening to the sacred lands of Avalon.

Even among the half-million people, we would bump into people we knew as we wandered around the vastness of the festival site, music pumping. Overwhelmed with love everywhere, overwhelmed with a sense of being home, I stood staring at The Pyramid for the first time, watching David Bowie singing "China Girl." There it was again... *euphoria.*

Harry tapped me on the shoulder.

"Come here, you need to see this!"

He lifted me onto his shoulders like an all-powerful giant. I looked out at the greatest sight I had ever seen: miles and miles and miles of twinkling lights, a sea of hundreds of thousands of lighters and flares in the air, the Pyramid stage glowing bright, the Glastonbury Tor in the distance, and the Starman himself singing into my heart. A lightning bolt went through my body. Energy flowed fast like a river. I was overwhelmed with a sense of love and unity. I could feel my connection to the lands, to the people, to the universe, to something bigger than me. *I'm a part of this. All of this! Everything is connected. We were all one. It's all just love!* As I basked in this new energy flowing through me, making the fine hairs on my skin stand on end and my body convulse, I sobbed tears of love and gratitude. I knew something inside was never going to rest again until this feeling was no longer just a fleeting moment but a way of life.

I cried for weeks after. I wanted to go *back home*, back to the lands of Glastonbury. I now *knew* there was something more. I had felt that *something* I'd been seeking since I was a little girl staring at the stars. The inner free spirit had been activated. I was ready for what was coming. I just didn't know what it would be.

We wrapped up the summer of 2000, packed in our jobs at the pub, moved to London with our friends, and went off to seek our fortunes. We landed on our feet and found ourselves a luxury apartment that was way out of our league, huge with cream walls and carpets, two balconies and views overlooking the city! We were clueless and simply assumed we'd just find work that would cover the extortionate rent. And somehow we did. We lived on next to no money, surviving on temp jobs that paid almost nothing.

But we always had a full pack of cigarettes on the counter, a bottle of champagne in the fridge, a bag of peas in the freezer, and a party every weekend full of awesome friends. Somehow, I seemed to have gotten that lovely home I had always wanted.

***

The messenger

The summer had awakened the old hippy heart of mine and now I was seeking more. There are always people who come into our lives to be conduits for the information we need. There will always be someone who holds a key to a door we need to travel through.

Nick was not seemingly the most spiritual of people, more like the kamikaze brother I never had. I found him equally wonderful as I did annoying. One of Harry's close friends from school, we immediately bonded when we met, and he became my brother from another mother. Nick was fun and mischievous, but his desire to push boundaries unnerved me. The first time I got in a car with him, he told me casually that he didn't have his licence yet. I was a lover of breaking the rules, but not the law. I had all the traits of a free spirit, but was well-conditioned enough to fear being put in a cell!

Nick's adventures meant he was always seeking more meaning in his life. He was spiritual and curious, but sometimes found himself distracted with a crowd that were the polarity of his seeker side, distracting him from his deeper wisdom, the wisdom I loved. He would turn up with a crystal around his neck and new stories of where he'd been traveling in Africa, what it was like, where he'd been living on a beach with no-one around. He was wild and free in ways I could only dream. Harry and I wanted to travel, but couldn't raise the funds because we were too busy going out drinking every night. And in truth, the thought of living *that* wild scared the crap out of me.

"Lou, you have to read this book called *The Celestine Prophecy*," Nick announced for the millionth time that year. I'd so far resisted his constant drive to tell me I should read this book.

"To be honest, Nick, the title sounds too complicated for my head."

I struggled with books at the best of times, but that one was intimidating. I felt inferior. The words seemed too big. *'Celestine' — what does that even mean? 'Prophecy' — sounds like something from a philosophy class I'm too thick to take!*

Nick laughed, "Lou, it's easy. I promise you'll love it. Just go get a copy."

The issues I had with my intellect ran deep. I had a ground-in belief that I was not clever enough to read anything other than bitesize trashy novels, so I certainly didn't have the intellect to digest a book called *The Celestine Prophecy.*

Finally, one day, Nick brought a copy to our new flat and, after ignoring it for weeks, I began to read it on the Tube and during the lunch breaks at my soul-destroying temp jobs. Sitting on reception desks in the City was a far cry from my dreams of being an event manager in the music industry, but with this book, I was finally understanding myself. After work, I would lie in bed with Harry, wrapped in his arms, reading. Something made him take notice. I sensed it was awakening his own long-held desires to go to Peru. We had agreed we would save up and go one day, but we were yet to open a savings account, let alone put money aside.

"It's about a man on a mission to find hidden manuscripts in Peru. He talks about how everything just *happened* for him, how the right people came at the right time, how there are no coincidences, and how humans feed and drain each other's energy. He says it's possible to give and receive energy. We have these different aspects of ourselves that began in childhood that we use to manipulate each other, and gain power, energy and control between each other."

I explained the four roles that the book had described, which people used to play their control dramas. There was The Intimidator, a kind of person who used fear and threats to get people to pay attention. I had a boss at the time who scared the shit out of me every time he walked into the office because he was so intimidating. Then there was The Interrogator, who stole energy by finding faults in others and making them feel inferior or inadequate by judging or questioning them. My mind flitted to my real dad and a flashback of my entire childhood played out in my mind. It was as if he couldn't help himself; he had to criticise me and my brothers. The Aloof was the person who acted coy and shy to gain energy and attention from people. These people didn't give anything away and acted clueless. My mind went to a guy at work whose aloofness triggered me, so much so I would overcompensate by being extra nice to him, trying to make him like me because I feared he hated me! And then there was The Poor Me, who took energy by making people feel guilty and complaining about problems without stating solutions. This one reminded me of myself.

I'd fallen victim to victims all my life, trying to rescue everyone who felt the world was being unkind to them, who felt they had pulled the short straw. I was the one who would give up my bed, my money and all of my time for those who played that card. I just wanted to make them feel better. At the time, I had no awareness that being a rescuer kept the victim in their place. It wasn't empowering them as I thought; it was enabling them to stay a victim. Still, it would be years before I gathered enough awareness of how these control dramas impacted me and could make shifts in my life.

The book talked about how these four roles controlled and manipulated situations and people, rather than people coming from a place of integrity, balance and harmony. I had felt this all my life. I could feel people's intentions and see through their lies.

The book also touched on those strange coincidences that happen in life. I couldn't recall many, but I knew I'd said "that's freaky" to friends when we called each other at the same time or bumped into old mates in random places.

The last part of the book that caught my attention was energy. How we all have energy fields that are possible to see. It reminded me of staring at the moon and stars when I was little and waiting to see something more. Or being at Glastonbury and seeing everything was connected. I knew there was something deeper that I wasn't fully seeing yet.

Harry thought it was a load of crap, of course, and would take the piss out of me for reading such hippy trash. He would snog my face off just to shut me up, but I didn't want sex that night. I wanted to talk about the deeper meaning of life. Nick's book was like a doorway to a world I felt sure I had once known but had somehow forgotten along the way. I was smitten with the book, and escaped into it and into the world my soul knew all along. I wanted to feel and see what the character was feeling. In my bones, I knew it was possible for me too because it felt so familiar.

One evening, I asked Nick about the prophecies that the book taught and why it wasn't in the news. He laughed in shock that I'd believed it was real.

"The book isn't true, Lou. It's just the ideas that are."

I felt ashamed. Naivety had gotten the better of me, once again. Yet I still knew what was happening in the book was possible for me too: to connect deeper into the world, to feel into the energy, to make amazing coincidences happen. More and more of them from my own life came to mind and I remembered being led to places and people.

"Harry, the times when you used to come into the pub and that song was always playing, or the times when we're thinking the same thing, are you saying it's all coincidence?"

"Yes, Lou, totally random. It happens. It's just life!" He would roll his eyes.

"What about the time I ran away from that crazy boss at the temp job who I thought was going to attack me? Right when I arrived at the recruitment offices in tears and they sat me down with a cup of tea, a job doing music for adverts at a recording studio two streets away came through. Even the guy said, 'This is so weird. It's like this job was written for you.' I'd done my dissertation on that *exact thing*. I was given the job on the spot 20 minutes later. That's no way a coincidence!"

"Yes, it is," Harry replied blankly, not looking up from his car magazine.

His resistance got under my skin.

***

Peeking through the veils

I gazed into the vagueness of the crowd on the Tube, drifting into a space of nothing, and sucking my thumb. I still did this, even at 21 years old. It was like meditation for me; a calmness would come and I would be in a space of no thoughts, simply watching everything in the moment as it happened. I was beyond caring what people thought about my thumb-sucking. I needed it!

Something made me look up from the floor of the carriage. Sitting nearby me was a guy and there was a purple light all around his knee. *What the fuck?* I kept closing and opening my eyes to see if it would move and work out what it was. *Must be a reflection or my eyes going funny.* I blinked hard, but it was still there. I blinked again and looked around the Tube then brought my eyes back to his legs. The purple light was still there! I bubbled with excitement and became more alert. Something had woken up. I could see something at last. *But what is it? Why only this guy? Why can't I see it on anyone else?* The light disappeared as soon as I began to think about it...

I told Harry about my experience and was surprised by his openness to it. Later, though, when we met our gang in the pub and told them about the purple light, Harry gave all these scientific reasons as to why it could happen. I was cross with him for squashing my experience down because I knew what I'd seen. A few months earlier, he'd joined me and Nick socially on a ganja-smoking aura-staring evening and had been open-minded. He would go back and forth in his views on alternative thinking, depending on who we were hanging out with at the time. It would piss me off, but I was used to Harry's mind opening and closing.

I was certain in my own mind about seeing the purple aura, though. And then it happened again...

***

We headed off to Crete that summer with a gang of friends. One night, I got so drunk that I puked black sambuca all over the cab and myself. The next day, I was tender, broken, hardly able to move. That evening's shenanigans ended early for me, because I was ruined by dinnertime and just wanted to go home. Everyone else was having a good time, but Nick offered to take me back and do some Reiki on me. I didn't even know what that was, but if it saved me from my hangover hole and involved me lying down, Nick could do whatever he liked!

A few months earlier, Nick had met a crystal shop owner, who taught him about energy. He kept telling me I needed to go and see this guy and learn Reiki myself, but at £150, the course was the total of my monthly disposable income at the time. And I valued smoking and going out above all else.

We got home and I rested lengthways on the bed. Nick sat on the floor and cupped my head with his hands. I was so glad to just lie down and it felt good to not be alone in my hungover pain. I closed my eyes and relaxed into the warmth of Nick's hands. The darkness in my eyes began to expand, as if I could see for miles through the dark. Then it opened up and I was *flying* through space, stars everywhere. It was beautiful, but over far too soon.

Nick headed back out with the boys, leaving me to sleep and drift into new places inside of myself. Here I was, beginning to awaken...

***

CHAPTER 4

BREAK FROM THE NORM

Creating comfort

IT WAS 2002 AND fear of an out-of-control property market guided us to move out of London, so we could save to buy a little flat. Getting on the property ladder was becoming an impossible dream that was getting further and further away from us. Even renting meant we were unable to put money aside. We moved five times that year in an attempt to find cheap rent and start saving. I was fed up.

But in a strange and beautiful moment, I saw it was no coincidence, as I found myself one Sunday afternoon staring at an aerial photo of Harry's parents' house, surrounded by other properties. Harry's dad explained that he had built this house next door to grandad, who had built his house next door to great-grandma, who had died many years ago.

"That's a cool house," I said, feeling drawn to it.

"I hate that house," Harry replied, "It's dark and cold, and feels horrible. I don't think I've been in there since I was two years old."

Sensing my strong pull towards it, Harry's dad jumped in.

"The tenants have lived there for years. The property is nothing to do with us now."

I brushed off the slight embarrassment, like a little girl who'd been caught looking at a piece of cake that wasn't hers.

"Wow! So your great-gran lived next to your nan and grandad. And your parents live next door to your grandad now. That's so lovely," I said, deflecting the shame with as much joy in my voice as I could manage.

Two days later, Harry's great-grandma's house had not crossed my mind again, when the phone rang. It was Harry's grandad next door calling to say his neighbours had just handed in their notice after 10 years of living there.

"Do you want to move in? You could get it for reduced rent," his grandad asked.

"A coincidence, right, Harry?" I teased.

A pretty little place in its own unique way, the house was detached, with four front windows and a door in the middle, just like I would draw as a girl. Harry resisted. It was indeed dark and cold. It was old and hadn't been decorated since the war. So old, in fact, that it only had an outdoor loo! I fell in love with it immediately.

"It's only for a short time, Harry, until we save some money. And it will be fun to be so close to your family. Plus, we can have *really* loud parties because it's detached."

Harry wasn't convinced, but we were living in our friend's spare room, which couldn't go on forever. He gave in. He didn't have much choice.

The day we moved in, I cried from exhaustion. Shifting our furniture five times in a year broke me.

"I'm never moving again! Ever!" I announced, not knowing then how powerful those words would be.

With our limited budget, we painted and decorated the best we could, and made the house our home. Albeit one with ice on the inside of the windows, mould in every room, threadbare carpets, and a questionable kitchen and bathroom.

***

Two years later at 24 years of age, I barefooted it down the aisle of a semi-derelict manor house with a dad on each arm.

Beyond the long, regal and beautifully finished main hall, where the sun streamed through the floor-to-ceiling windows, flooding light on smiling faces and teary eyes, were 100 bare-brick rooms awaiting renovation. I was the pioneer bride to walk down this aisle. Many would follow me, but I first dared to trust a space that was far from the norm, and it worked in ways I could never have dreamed. The juxtaposition of polished and understated was a metaphor of my own soul's journey and its limitless potential. I wanted to be different, to push for new ways of being and be the first to try them, to forge my own path and step into journeys no-one had walked before.

I felt an affinity to this place, its unique energy calling to become something greater than its current state. It spoke to the innocence within me, a childhood awareness within my heart that our world was full of infinite possibilities and the deeper truth that anything can grow into something spectacular when nurtured with love. I knew this to be true in my relationship with Harry. I knew it to be true with my friendships. And I longed for it to be true in my inner world.

To most people's annoyance and frustration, I was learning be who I truly was and seeing that I wouldn't get rejected and judged by people if I gently bucked the norm. There were choices to make and I saw that my decisions had to be in line with my true self rather than what was best for other people. Subtly, I began resisting rules that narrowed the path towards the conventional. Refusing to conform, I would not become another cog in the clock, another rat in the race, another brick in the wall.

Harry was my polarity. The yang to my yin, the science to my mysticism, the rules to my creative free spirit, the firm resistance to my wilful wildness. He wanted to hold my hand and lead us down a safe path many had walked before us, where there was less fuss, less attention, less judgment. The path of comfort, the familiar path, the normal path, where normal people walked, the one that was proven to work. But his faith in me, his unwavering love, his deep knowing that he would not and could not live without me meant he knew there would be times he had to let go of safety and welcome surprise. My love and faith in him meant, sometimes, on occasions, in rare circumstances, if he absolutely dug his heels in, I would honour his need for stillness, security and the status quo!

Our friends basked in the hot sun outside the marquee, laughing, playing around like children. The boys got on all fours and I hitched up my dress and clambered up Harry's back to create a human triangle, giggling, tumbling on top of each other, my boobs falling out. I didn't care. No-one cared. We didn't fear judgment or comply with etiquette. These guys and girls, they were our blood, our glue, our vitality, our adventure, our tribe. Harry and I found strength because we were surrounded by people who loved us unconditionally. We chose friends who rooted for us, respected us and honoured us. When the walls got crumbly, they were always there with us to sort it out, rather than adding to the load or destabilising our foundation. *Hear no evil, see no evil, speak no evil.*

We humans meet the energy of the company we keep, and Harry and I kept great company, discerning who matched our values of kindness, love, fun and adventure. The energy flow between friends and family was effortless and reciprocal, and I learned to find friends who chose love over the love of drama.

At the end of the evening under the stars, the warmth of the summer air soft on our skin, I showed my family just what we got up to with our friends. Hiking up the skirt of my wedding dress and displaying my dirty henna-tattooed feet, I grabbed a huge African drum and stuck it between my legs. Accompanied by five of my friends and our drum teacher, the tribal beats came together. The energy was rising. The guests were drawn in close to the show. The family gathered, old and young, and I watched their faces glowing in awe. Next, three of my bridesmaids lit their *fire poi*, something all our friends had mastered over the years. The flames danced around their heads and bodies, their eyes bright, their rhythms in time to the drums. They captivated every one of our guests with golden circles in the night sky.

Tears filled my eyes. In my own trance, time slowed. I was overawed with love and gratitude. These were our tribes coming closer, family and friends, a moment in time where all the people we loved were together. United.

***

Leap, my darling, and the net will appear

Once again, my need to break norms was reflected in our honeymoon choice. We landed after our five-day honeymoon in Ibiza, where we'd seen more of our hotel room by day than by night, and jumped straight into our car for our now-annual party pilgrimage to the West Country. It was to be another five days of hedonism with our friends. As ever, Glastonbury was the gateway to a summer filled with more festivals, more parties, more living for the weekend and more checking out of reality. By August bank holiday, when I realised there were no further festivals, weddings or weekenders to keep me distracted, a darkness crept in. A fear of stopping. What was my life now the parties were over?

I had to face the fact I was spending most of my life sitting on the A40 into London going to a crappy admin job at a shopping channel that paid next to nothing and drained my energy, pulling me away from my dreams of working in the music industry. I knew there was more to life than this. On top of that feeling, my boss was bullying me and I was growing increasingly anxious every day, making my dyslexia worse and mistakes happen more regularly as I trod on eggshells around him. Even though I looked the same as anyone else on the outside, on the inside, I was different. I didn't want to join in the bitching. The back-stabbing and cut-throat culture was a far cry from where my free spirit wanted to be.

I began to get sadder and worry flooded my body each morning. I wrapped myself into Harry, dreading the moment he would get out of bed to catch his train into London. From the moment my eyes opened, anxiety would take over my body, fear that something bad was going to happen.

Every night, I came home heavy after work. We'd eat food that made me fat. I'd watch soap operas in one room, while Harry would watch football in another. I'd drink half a bottle of wine, smoke 20 cigarettes, and become victim to my own negative language. I blamed work and colleagues for my stuckness. I blamed the lack of other work options on the recession. I talked about how we would never be able to buy a house. I found all the reasons out there that life was hard. Then I would wake up in the morning, wrap myself into Harry, and start worrying something bad was going to happen all over again.

It was like *Groundhog Day*. I was even bored of myself!

If I didn't want to go to work, I would make myself sick so I could justify staying in bed and hiding from the world, which was all I wanted to do. I lost all connection to my hippy heart.

One day, as Nick was listening to me moan about how hard it was to get a job, he said I was turning into a Poor Me.

"No, I'm not! I'm always *radiating* energy!" I snapped back, not wanting to see my own behaviour. "I look out for other people. I'd do anything for anyone. I'm the life and soul of the party. I'm not a Poor Me." I insisted.

With a deep sigh, he replied, "Lou, you're a Poor Me. All you talk about is how hard it is to get a job, how your boss is awful to you, how there isn't any work anywhere, how you can't afford to get on the property ladder and how much tidying up you have to do!" He suggested I re-read *The Celestine Prophecy*.

The message slammed me in my heart. I was taken aback and went off to the kitchen to get a drink. I knew what he was saying had an element of truth to it. I knew I could either get pissed off with him or try to learn something. I could see he was right, so I took a breath and went back to the conversation, as gracefully as I could. I wasn't off the hook. Nick didn't let up. Then Harry jumped in.

"You've become a real bitch lately. When you go to the pub with that new friend of yours, all you do is drop to her level and bitch about other people."

I felt attacked, but they had a point. I had become that. There was this one friend who I'd see weekly outside my main circle. I valued and loved her, but she was bitchy and would tell me I was too nice. In time, I found it easier to join in with her judgments and projections about people. Talking about others had become a way of being accepted by her. Even though in my heart it felt deeply uncomfortable and I knew she only did it because she felt shit about herself, I found myself more and more sucked in, because I wanted to be part of her gang.

Harry was right, and Nick was right, but I needed time to think about it. And during that time, I was going to hate them both for a while! I wanted them to feel bad for upsetting me, so I went off upstairs and sulked. When I came back downstairs, Nick joined me as I was having a cigarette.

"Lou, you've gotta quit this shit. It's no good for you. I've heard you can smoke until you're 25, but then you've got to regain your lungs or you'll ruin your body. Quit the fags, get some exercise, stop eating all those crappy cheesecakes and watching rubbish on TV. And would you just fucking leave your job already. Stop looking for problems. Find some solutions. I hate seeing you like this!"

I had to admit I had been like that — bitchy and moany — even speaking to Harry in ways I hated to hear women talk to their men, that derogatory, eye-rolling way, the passive aggressive way, the way everyone seems to think is okay, but I knew was not nice. I couldn't bear hearing women complain about their men, colluding about what they did and didn't do. Yet I had become that very person. And the more I became this way, the more it made us both miserable and argumentative.

It had to stop. I had to stop, because this was how women in my family spoke to their men, and that was not how I wanted to be. I wanted to become more conscious. I wanted to hear the language I was using. I wanted to stop being such a victim. I wanted to change the behaviour I'd started seeing in myself. I wanted to own who I truly was and not change myself for other people.

When I was growing up, my stepdad would say, "A man in the ranks will stay in the ranks, because he doesn't have the ability to get things done." That phrase would whirl around my head as I willed myself out of bed. Was I destined to stay in the ranks because I couldn't get my arse into gear? I needed to find a way out, but I kept getting stuck. I'd been looking for something new but didn't seem to get any interviews. The autumn leaves were falling and I had to shed this job, like the trees were shedding. Nothing was going to get any better without doing something. If I was ever going to achieve my lofty ideals of big houses and flashy sports cars, something would need to change!

So, with Michael Jackson playing in the background, I set the intention to see myself. I would take a look at the woman in the mirror and *choose* to make a change. Any change! Starting with my job. I didn't want to be there and they didn't want me there. It was time to go.

I handed in my notice with no idea of what was next and my mind, body and energy changed within a matter of days. My hair shone, I lost some weight, my skin radiated, my libido picked up, and I was feeling good about myself. I was back in my power! Four weeks later, I left my job on a high, waving a sweet 'fuck you' and pretending I'd landed some kickass events job in the City, even though I hadn't.

One week after that, my bravado came crashing down. I stared out the window of our freezing spare room thinking, *What the fuck have I done?* We were already living hand-to-mouth every month. Losing my wage was going to hit us hard. My mind went into every possible scenario of how shit everything was going to be. I wrapped myself in a duvet and let all the stories flood back in, dipping back into Poor Me.

No-one will want me... I'm not clever enough... There aren't any jobs for me... It's so hard... It's not fair... I'm too old now... My time has passed... I'm destined to end up in another crap job.

I knew this was the wrong mindset, but with no-one around, I found it hard to motivate myself. I carried on applying for jobs in the event industry but getting no bites.

I could hear my stepdad in my ears. *Find solutions, not problems, Lou.* I managed to get some shifts at our local pub to pay a few bills, and that was when something started to happen. I lightened up a bit. I got an on-the-spot offer for an event officer job at a local high-end hotel. It wasn't quite right for me though. Something deep down was calling me to trust, to hold out a little longer, so I turned them down! It was crazy, but I called them just hours after they'd made the offer. On impulse later that afternoon, I applied for some free work experience. It felt a bit shameful, offering to do a student work placement at 25, but I told myself to get over it and act on this hunch. *Just get your foot in the door*, I said to myself. Within 24 hours, I had an interview in London at an event entertainment booking agency! I was buzzing.

Down a cobbled mews was a trendy little office with a handful of people working there, one of whom was a guy I'd gone to uni with. I got the placement and worked for free for two weeks before they offered me three days a week paid. Within two months, I was full-time booking circus skills, acrobats, actors and actresses for TV, ads and events. I loved the creative vibe and my whole outlook changed. I became the person I'd always known I was but could never find. I was confident and became pretty good at my work.

One day, my boss looked over his computer and said with a confused look on his face, "That's strange. You're never going to guess what email has just come in. They're asking us to manage production of the Urban Music Awards. They want a meeting. Why on earth are they emailing us? We do circus skills!"

But I was jumping around like Super Mario on giant mushrooms. I'd known this was the direction I wanted ever since I'd been to The BRIT Awards and joked to my best friend Sandy, "The only thing I want to do is run around backstage of an awards ceremony with a clipboard looking important." Somehow, this was now an achievable dream.

"This so happens to be the one and only job I have ever wanted to do in my entire life!" I squealed, "We have to do this!"

My boss laughed.

"Nothing ventured, nothing gained, I suppose!"

A week later, we found ourselves at a meeting in Hackney in some shabby yet welcoming offices, comprising a radio station, magazine, and various media outlets. I instantly liked the guy whose event it was. He was an entrepreneur with a million things on the go. It was a meeting of energetic connection and we communicated in the same way, beyond words, with a faith in everything working out. It was going to be a win-win for everyone. Just before we left, something prompted me to ask the burning question.

"Just out of curiosity, where did you get our company's details because these aren't the kind of events we normally do, but weirdly both Stu and I have music management degrees?"

"I have no idea who gave them to me," Jordan thought about it for a moment, "Actually, I can't remember where I found you at all! I just followed my intuition and clearly you guys are right for the job."

"It was always my dream to do something like this," I laughed as we all shook hands. We left their offices, and I was dumbfounded, but tingling with vitality. Once again, I had confirmation that greater things were at play. I knew it was because I was beginning to have faith in taking the unconventional route. I was not going to change that for anyone any more. The road less travelled was the one that delivered the greatest gifts.

***

Domestic healing

At home, I was trying. After some time in my awesome job, I had a higher energy about me, but that conversion a few months earlier with Nick and Harry never really left me. I wanted to be a better person and live happily ever after. So I tried and tried, but it wasn't easy.

I would catch myself moaning about doing the cleaning. It was hard to stop myself, easier to blame someone else. Sometimes I just wanted Harry to acknowledge all I did around the house. Nonetheless, I reined in my mood. I learned that if I said thank you to Harry for what he *did do*, rather than moan about what he *didn't do*, I felt higher. I noticed the more I moaned at him for not doing anything around the house, the less he would do, and the more distance came between us. I had to accept that Harry was never going to be a romantic. I knew he loved me, but he was never going to sweep me off my feet, be the one who brought me flowers, or surprise me with dinner dates. In fact, I don't think we'd ever been on a date on our own in the entire time we'd been together. I came to terms with the fact he liked coming in from work and watching TV. No amount of bitching was going to change that.

"Lou, just because you want to come in and cook dinner doesn't mean I want that. I want to sit and chill out for a while, then I'll help, but if you want to do it now, that's your choice. My choice is to sit here for 10 minutes. Please can you just respect that for me?"

Harry had grown frustrated at me constantly asking him to help, but I learned to listen, and although it felt deeply unfair that I was cooking dinner while he was watching TV, I realised that married life was about meeting in the middle, not forcing anyone to do anything they didn't want to do. The more positive I became in my thoughts about it all, the better I felt. I began to see how controlling I could be at times. I liked things to happen when I wanted them to happen and had to *learn* that he was never going to cook me dinner or clean the house on command. I knew he loved me and would do anything for me, so I tried my best to let some things go, to not get so uptight, and to stop the control dramas. Interestingly, as he began to enjoy the freedom, I'd find him at my side chopping onions or washing up far more frequently. All I needed to do was let it be *his choice* and not be so spiky with my energy.

Life was no longer a financial struggle as it had been throughout our relationship. We had always had lots of fun but no money, so having even a little bit of money felt like a huge release for us. We were commuting into the City together and I had a job I loved. My mind was clearer and I was more at peace. But after the London bombing, there was something lingering between us, an unspoken tension in our relationship that went on for months. My awareness of my intuition had been validated, heightened even, and I wanted to talk about it, but Harry adamantly did not. It seemed to annoy him if I spoke about anything even slightly 'out there' that didn't have the backing of scientific evidence. The more I tried, the more he put up a wall. I knew it could create a separation between us if I let it, and I valued our relationship too much. I knew the intuitive stuff was challenging his scientific mind, just as his logical approach challenged my spiritual insight.

"It's just coincidence, Lou," he would say flatly, which I refused to accept. Deep down I knew there were too many things now. Too many so-called 'coincidences.'

Our tensions subsided over the summer again, as festivals and parties took the forefront as usual. However, now that I was more aware of being in-tune, I would exercise my intuition more. I'd pick up the house phone to call people and they were doing the same on the other end. I'd have hunches to get in touch with friends right when they needed me or were feeling low. I'd always had an interest in the weird and wonderful; I seemed to know stuff others didn't. Over the years, I'd learned to hide it, but now I just couldn't any more. I acted on these hunches more and more, but if I ever brought it up with Harry, it would build friction between us.

November came into sight, which meant the Urban Music Awards were only a few days away. My dream was coming true, but Harry was being off with me. I couldn't seem to do or say anything right. Every time I talked about the fast-approaching event, he would make patronising remarks about the urban culture being 'dodgy.' He even hinted that he didn't want me doing the event and we fell out when I asked him to come to the launch party.

"It's just another event that will lead to gang-on-gang fighting. Why would I want to go to that? Why do *you* even want to go to that?" he snapped at me.

My defences were up.

"I love my work, I love the event, I love the artists, I love the culture. You're being pretty un-fucking-supportive, Harry, and getting wrapped up in the bullshit media circus designed to incite fear!"

"Lou, you seem to forget that someone got shot at the event last year."

"They got shot in the car park. It wasn't in the awards."

"It's the same fucking thing and you know it!"

"Look, we're being cautious. We know we need to keep certain artists away from each other to keep the peace. We'll make sure that happens. There's nothing to worry about."

I was confident and had brought in a team of over 100 people to manage the flow of artists in the green room so that none of the gang rivals would bump into each other. I had faith and wasn't worried in the slightest. It annoyed me that Harry was.

Three nights before the event, I was feeling the pressure of having to get the final bits together and Harry dropped a bombshell over dinner.

"I think you need to back out of doing the Urbans, Lou. It's dangerous."

"Don't be ridiculous," I replied, "Why would I back out now? This is my actual dream coming true."

"You're stupid for doing this. You have no idea what you're getting into," Harry pressed.

"Yes, I fucking do. This job came to me. I'm *meant* to do this. I *know* I can do this," I insisted. "I'll be fine. Nothing is going to go wrong. Stop worrying about something that hasn't even happened."

"You have no control when guns and knives are involved. No-one has. How can you say you'll be fine? You don't know that!"

"Yes, I do, Harry! I really know! I just know, alright? So please stop trying to sabotage the one thing I can actually do. You're making this so hard for me. I need your support. I support you all the time. Please just trust me on this."

He ignored me and went on.

"You're being blind, Lou. Not everyone in the world is as nice as they are in your head. You're being naive and risking your life. You have no idea of the stuff that goes on," he said.

"Harry, don't patronise me. I've been organising this for nine months. I know what I'm doing."

I struggled to convey my certainty that it was safe and Harry really gave it to me.

"Look, you have no idea that I spend my life protecting you while you float around in your little Lou bubble, clueless as to what's going on in the real world. You don't see it, but I'm always looking out for you. This time I can't fucking protect you if you get yourself into a situation."

"You don't need to fucking protect me, Harry!" I screamed at him, "You didn't try to protect me when London was being fucking bombed four months ago, did you? So I don't know why you're trying to protect me now!"

Finally, my fury about the day of the bombing, the anger I had held inside and never spoken about, was released. It had been sitting under my skin for all that time and now it was out.

"You've patronised me saying my intuition about the bombing was just coincidence, when I fucking *knew* something was wrong. You made me go into the City even though I *knew* something was going on. Then you fucked off to work and left me. You have no right to say you protected me. You didn't even listen to me. We could have been on that fucking bus and wound up dead if I hadn't jumped. And then you demean my intuition, as if I'm some airy-fairy idiot making something from nothing. When I asked you after the bombings if you would trust my intuition again, you told me you wouldn't and that it was just coincidence. I have learned to shut up about my intuition, but I'm not going to do that anymore. I have faith in this event. I have faith in me. And I'm fucking doing it whether you like it or not!"

I stormed off, grabbed my keys and left the house. It was something I never used to do, but since the bombings, it seemed to be okay to just leave in a blaze of rage! I drove down the motorway far too fast but realised I could hurt someone if I kept taking my anger out on the road. I slowed down and gathered my thoughts. I looked at it from his perspective, turning it over in my mind.

He does protect me all the time. I know he always looks out for me. The bombing day was a weird day. I can't bring all that into this, although I'm glad I said it. It felt good to say and I'm obviously still angry about it, because we've never talked about it. He always shuts down when I try. Why does he do that? I wonder if he feels bad. I need to let go of the bombings thing. He's never going to talk about it. I need to get him to be okay with the event.

If it was the other way around, maybe I'd be fearful too. I know all he wants to do is protect me. Falling out with me is just his way of stopping me from doing the event, his strategy to keep me safe, in the same way I was trying to protect him on the day of the bombings. This event has magically come to me. I know something godly is looking out for me. I feel like I'm being protected by something divine, but 'divine' is not a logical reason to feel safe in Harry's world.

I battled in my mind between who was right and who was wrong, but I knew my love for him was more important than this argument. I returned home half an hour later ready to speak with him. He was waiting at the door. His huge big brown eyes met mine, no words needed. He opened his arms, wrapped them around me, and held me tight.

"Lou, I'm sorry, I really am. I'm just so damn scared something will happen to you."

"I know. I'm sorry too, babe."

"No, I'm the one who needs to be sorry. You're right. I've been unsupportive. Fear of losing you is getting in the way of your dreams and I've been a real dick."

He took my face in his hands, looked at me and said with certainty, "I know you're going to be amazing, babe. You've got this."

I cried with relief into his chest. A weight had lifted. We made love that night, knowing that we were as fragile as we were strong, reclaiming what we had damaged between us by going deep into our souls. His eyes locked onto mine and I sensed he was still holding a slight fear. It was as if he was holding me over an abyss, afraid of letting me go. My arms wrapped tightly around his neck, willing him to hear my own certainty that we were safe. As we moved, the flow of our sexual healing travelled through us. Passionately, intensely, we let go of our fears with every breath, allowing past pains to release and transform. As we went deeper into each other, we surrendered. Our bodies communicated the familiar signals to each other, leading us to our sacred place where our energies met. I moved on top of him, looking down, this powerful stance raising us higher. He put his hands on my hips, holding me, breathing in unison, as the energy between us released simultaneously and the waves engulfed us.

The sweat trickled down my back, as I caught my breath. I leaned back, still feeling him inside me, and smiled at the peace in his eyes. Something pulled my attention outside the window. It was the brightest star in my favourite constellation, the only one I had ever actually known, The Seven Sisters. It felt like something magical was happening all around me.

We had reunited. We were starting to see each other again.

***

CHAPTER 5

THE UNIVERSE TAKES THE LEAD

Curveballs and creations

"HARRY!" I SHOUTED. *Fuck, fuck, fuck, fuck, fuck.* Harry appeared at the doorway of the bedroom. I looked up at him, my whole body shaking, scared. What did it mean? I didn't know what it meant.

The pregnancy test had showed the reading so quickly that I hadn't had time to digest what a cross or a line meant. I threw the peed-on stick over to him. "Does that cross mean I'm pregnant? Fuck, I think it means I'm fucking pregnant."

Fuck, fuck, fuck.

He held it in his shaking hands, fumbling the sheet of extensive instructions.

"What does it mean, babe?"

"I don't know, Lou! Give me a chance!"

"I think a cross means positive."

"Well then, probably it means you're pregnant."

"Oh Jesus, what are we going to do, babe?" I said.

Harry walked out of the room and down the stairs in a trance.

"Get rid of it then!" he threw back.

And in that moment, I laughed. He didn't mean it and it was enough to shake the fear out of me.

"I'm 26 years old and married to the love of my life, knobhead. I don't think we're getting rid of this baby," I exclaimed, more for my own benefit than for his.

"Looks like we're having a fucking baby then," he shouted back up the stairs.

Our world did a full 360 in 0.8 seconds. I reached the bottom of the stairs after him with tears of joy falling down my cheeks. I could see Harry smiling. Like two children looking desperately for an adult, we sat in the doctor's surgery 20 minutes later on an emergency appointment. Dipping a strip into my wee sample, the doctor beamed over her half-moon glasses, "Looks like you're *very* pregnant."

We laughed and stuttered, "What do we do now?"

Handing me a red folder, she said, "This will be your file from now on. The midwives will call you in a few weeks to see how you're getting on."

As we walked into the waiting room, I held that red folder proudly so everyone could see.

Suddenly, dreams of travelling the world together, fears of not being able to grow our careers, and worries about saving for a mortgage didn't seem so important anymore. I looked for the silver lining and assumed this curveball had wiped out our plans for a greater reason, not just because of our dubious ideas that we didn't need to use condoms around my period! I was so excited I couldn't put my mind to anything other than being pregnant. It consumed my every thought when I felt well and it consumed my whole body when I felt waves of nausea!

Six weeks after we found out, the scan showed that this baby was due on my 27th birthday, which triggered a clear memory of a conversation we'd had when we first got together. We had agreed that 27 was a good age to have a baby, though at 17, of course, 27 seemed a lifetime away. I realised that we plant seeds that make things happen long before they materialise. We make remarks so flippantly at the time, but they drift into the universe like spells and come back as reality.

***

I got off the train, proudly showing the tiniest of 16-week bumps under my skin-tight dress. I wanted the whole world to see that I had a little life growing inside of me. I felt like the most special human being in the world.

The man who cleaned the loos at the train station beamed at me. He could have been 40 or 70; I couldn't tell and it didn't matter. All I knew was that he was a beautiful soul and made me feel joyful in a time when I was having to rethink grand plans. His smile taught me that life is so much more than our job. It's how we make people *feel* that's important, what we give to the world. We could be the best paid lawyer in Moorgate or this guy scrubbing the sinks at Marylebone, but what defines us is our openness, our choices, our values, what we give back to society and how true we are to ourselves. Who we are as people, that's what counts.

I was starting to see that our jobs do not define us as humans. Yes, our jobs lead us to greater parts of ourselves, challenging us to go deeper. In fact, my job had often taught me how to grow within myself and shown me that I had courage, integrity, faith. On some level, I'd begun to have more trust in myself. I felt capable of being good at something. I also understood my job made me look cool, which gave me a sense of worth. I loved the moment people asked me what I did, their reactions when I told them. It made me feel successful, on the surface. Yet there was always an underlying feeling of being a fraud, though I masked it well, even from myself.

As I watched this guy cleaning day after day, I saw he was truly happy. He didn't seem to care what people thought of him, which meant no-one could judge him. He was so confident in himself. I respected him and he respected everyone. I was a long way off that feeling but I knew I wanted to be like him. His gift to the world was to fill hearts with love and connection, reminding commuters that we were human. Beyond our suits, beyond our salaries and badges of importance, we were all the same. When I smiled back at him, I reciprocated the love he had given me. I wondered how many people he made feel that way every day, how many other people headed to the bathrooms to see his warm beam and say good morning.

I knew everyone would have their opinion on any changes I made over the next few months, but I had to shut them down and keep their well-meaning ideas away so they didn't interfere with my own inner guidance. It was clear to me that everyone else's advice was based on who *they* were and not on who *I* was. Yes, they made logical sense, but it was obvious I could not and would not walk anyone else's path. Logical choices kept me in chains. Choices made from my heart, without too much thinking, led me to places and people that were incredible, even seemingly impossible. Not only that, but my intuition was getting louder, the more confident I became. *Sometimes we all have to break away from what we know, so we can see what's out there for us*, I thought to myself.

"We just have to have this faith that everything will work out," I announced to Harry back at home.

"It's okay to not know what we need to do," I continued. "Maybe we just do what we feel is right for now and see where it leads us. Our minds may never know what our purpose is in this world, but *something* inside does."

Curled up in our little house, I just had to let it unfold. Let go and trust. Other people's fears made me trust myself less, so I would put up my force fields and ignore their worries, tuning into my own knowing. I didn't want to be limited in choosing what I wanted for my life. And I knew I wanted to raise this baby myself. Often we want for our children what we never had growing up. For me, that was having a stay-at-home mum.

There was no other option: I had to set up a business I could do from home. And it had to be successful. And it had to change the world. And it had to make people feel like the guy cleaning the loos at the station.

***

We had booked a ski holiday the year before. In the past, my parents had always paid for our ski holidays. This was the first time we had paid for ourselves, so I had no intention of cancelling. I was a good skier. It had been 'my thing' since childhood and the only skill I *knew* I could nail. By this time, I had a 20-week baby in my belly and a fire inside that said

I could do anything. I had no fear. Something else was guiding me, something powerful, something divine.

The mountains gave me space to think, feel, and simply be. I reflected on who I was: sentimental, nostalgic, a lover of special memories. For me, it was key to feel magical moments deep inside, journaling about them, sharing them. Soundtracking photos and videos with music blew my mind. I was the friend who would make montages for everyone's birthdays, or huge memory books with stories and pictures. I wanted people to feel what I felt: a love of friends, family and truly living. I saw life in pictures, then music would take me deeper. Archiving these moments made me feel grateful, knowing I could die tomorrow and would have lived...

As I watched the world go by outside the mountain resort, I put my hand on my belly and the baby moved. I felt a connection from deep in my belly to the mountains, to the sky, to my family sitting around me, all the way to the sun. I soaked it in and drifted off in reflection. I wanted a world for my child where everyone looked out for each other, where strangers helped one another. It made me weep to see kindness and I was dedicated to a world where everyone saw the deep sacredness and joy of their life. Most of all, I needed to leave a legacy for my child. When we know we have to leave a legacy for our children, when we know life is short, we don't waste time in jobs we hate. We always find a way, solutions not problems, more time to do what we love and help others. When we aren't afraid of our own mortality, we face it rather than fear it, celebrate life every day. We make peace with people, stronger bonds, better marriages. We don't take people and resources for granted. We look beyond the dramas, the need to control and blame, and all live blessed, wonderful lives together.

"Oh, you've always been such a softie, Lou. Life isn't like it appears through your rose-tinted glasses," Mum told me.

"I know life can be hard and I know I'm blessed, but it's not a given that everyone has to be a slave to a system! We don't have to do what we think we have to do, then die regretting never doing anything we actually wanted or knew we were put here to do!"

I loved everyone in my life, but endearing 'typical Lou' eye-rolling was something they shared. Even done jokingly and out of love, it was keeping me in a box, making me small without them even realising they were doing it. I was fed up of feeling like no-one quite believed I could do it. And now this...

"It's not the right time to set up a business when you've got a baby on the way."

I often sensed people thought I couldn't handle responsibility. Which was enough motivation to make me act. *I'll prove it to them!* The knowing of life and the knowing of death was loud inside of me. I knew I was so deeply in love with Harry because he could be gone in a moment. I was deeply in love with life for the same reason. I had to leave this life having been the best version of myself. This pregnancy was awakening a need to leave a legacy. And that legacy was for me to give back to the world.

I would create that in my business and help people leave a legacy of their own. That was what I was gonna do!

***

Following the threads of 'something'

I came back from skiing, quit my job, then followed the threads. I created ideas from what was inside. 'Something' in me whispered, *Remind people of the sacredness of life. Help them see their blessings in the many small moments. When people see how beautiful their lives are, it will help them die peacefully one day and those who are left behind will be able to let go with joy.*

I listened to whatever was guiding my many seemingly mad ideas and settled on... an event production company for funerals! It was the beginning of the apprenticeship for my life purpose, but I wasn't to know this until much further down the line. I had a long way to go before I truly understood the ramblings of my inner voice, the 'something' inside. Many more lessons, many more discoveries. I had to go deeper into myself, the world and the Universe.

There is no way our minds can know where our hearts and souls are guiding us. There is no way our imagination or even dreams can tell what the future has in store. All we need to do is follow the threads, one by one. If only we knew that every step led by our hearts, every leap made by our souls, are building blocks to a future unique to us. Our minds do not know the true reason we are on this earth, but our souls do.

I floated around in my pregnancy, starting to dip my toes in the waters of my own destiny. I had a new intuition, true inner guidance that spoke to me in a different way to the internal dialogues running riot in my mind most days. It was a voice that was wise and soothing. I was far from perfect at listening, but I knew it was there.

I found simple visualisations and breathing exercises just so bloody frustrating, but I stuck with them because they were helping. Instead of the old dialogues that played in the background, reminding me I wasn't enough, worrying that everything would go wrong, or telling me I was too stupid to run a business, they were words of encouragement. Faith!

The TV went off. I bought a desk. I worked on my new business from 7am until I went to bed. I was planning, discovering, playing with ideas. I had never found such focus and drive. I wouldn't stop. I was on fire.

"Lou, I want to invest £200 into your business. Go buy some business cards and get things rolling," Mum said.

She believed in me and my rose-tinted glasses after all! And so did everyone else. I put out emails to friends asking for help with names. They all got involved and I felt their pride in me.

"I don't know what's changed," I said to Harry in passing, "They all seem really behind me, like they have faith in me."

"It's because you have faith in you," he replied.

I thought about what he said. I *had* changed my view of myself. I *did* have faith in myself. I'd begun to believe in myself, so they began believing in me. All my life I had been looking for someone else to believe in me first, almost waiting for permission, yet all along it was simple. It had to come from me.

If I looked too closely at what I was doing, it could be overwhelming, but when I looked lightly, the potential was limitless. I learned to get on with things without thinking too much.

As well as growing my business, I was growing my baby and learning hypnobirthing. Plus, there was work being done on our house that wasn't actually getting done and making me cross. Tensions were high and some days I was not the blissed-out hippy mamma I wanted to be.

"Feel the colour red, like a warm mist all around you," said the soft voice on the birthing meditation, as I rested on the living room floor. But I could not for the life of me visualise the colour red; the more I tried, the more that red resisted! The peace and stillness it was meant to create was making me want to throw the fucking hypnobirthing CD out the window.

"Argh!"

I tried to get Harry's attention.

"Can you help me, Harry? Can you just help me do this meditation?" I urged, as if it was his fault I was finding it frustrating.

Harry came out of the office looking like a henpecked old man. Flatly, he took the birthing book from my hand and read out the words of the rainbow visualisation.

"Let yourself relax and breathe. Visualise the colour red--"

"Don't bother," I snapped.

"I don't know what else you want me to do, Lou," he sighed.

He was trying, but it was all a bit out there for him. Clearly, he felt the pressure of my expectations of him transforming into some perfect birthing partner. It wasn't his style at all, this hippy hypnobirthing stuff, and I knew it. Yet it still annoyed me. I could see he had decided that it wasn't for him and gone all awkward about it. *Why can't he just get over himself? This is the new millennium where dads get involved!*

At the time, I didn't think my expectations of him were too much to ask, and getting pissed off meant I pushed him in the opposite direction of what I wanted — a peaceful alternative birth. His way of defusing my overly erratic pregnancy hormones was to simply change the subject and walk away.

"Want a cup of that weird tea you drink?"

I wanted to hate him, blame him for everything that I felt was wrong in that moment, for not being the man who would read children's stories to my bump every night so the baby could hear his voice, or massage my neck without giving up after two seconds, or talk about the birth all the time. But that was defeating the whole point of the relaxation techniques and I needed to sort out my attitude.

"Yeah, raspberry leaf tea would be nice," I sighed.

I began the visualisation again, on my own, this time letting myself forget about getting the colour red and moving onto the other colours. The more I relaxed, the easier I could visualise each colour of the rainbow — soon even red! By the time my cup of tea arrived, I had drifted to the most blissful place, a new place of stillness that I wanted to feel more and more.

***

Already, my baby was changing me. Years of going to Glastonbury Festival had made me want to look after our planet, but more than ever I saw aspects of nature I had never seen before. I became aware of the earth. I wanted a chemical-free world. I wanted clean water. I knew we were killing the bees, and raising the oceans, and polluting the lungs of the earth. Yes, it was easier to ignore than to face making changes, but I didn't want any part in contributing to this kind of world where my child would live.

She was born in all the ways I had not planned. They lifted her from my cut belly on the operating table. I watched Harry take our screaming, bloody, slimy girl and tuck her into his blue hospital gown, skin to skin. She stopped crying, and he knelt down to show me her peaceful face scrunched into his chest. After all, the perfect daddy.

We named her Avalon, after the Fields of Avalon at Glastonbury. We knew she would never miss a festival.

"I'm gonna raise you differently, Avalon. We're going against the grain, baby," I promised. "I want to show you a different world, one where you can be completely you. And I hope to God I live long enough to teach you all you need to see you through this life."

For months, I revelled in the revealing of my daughter's spirit, every move, every smile, every day was a new day. As she grew, I grew. I looked on in awe and wonder as she peered at me with her mystical navy-blue eyes. She had more hair than a newborn ever should and looked remarkably like me as a baby but also just like Harry.

She was the golden baby for months, sleeping and feeding like an angel. Life was like a dream. The summer was hot, and all I had to do was make a few phone calls and send a few emails to keep the business ticking along while she suckled sweetly. I was a natural. I knew I was. There was a growing ego inside of me that fed from this perfection. I felt too proud of being a floaty, dreamy, hippy mamma whose child slept all night and fed like a dream. And not only a new mum, I was also running a new business. I felt important. Especially when it came to nappy advice.

I was conscious the world needed to change, but I could see the addictiveness and righteousness that came with it. I was on a one-woman mission to make a difference one nappy, one bottle, one organic potato at a time. Internally, I judged other mums who used disposable nappies, drank coffee while breastfeeding, or used branded chemical cleaners in their home. I was strong in my views and felt it my duty to educate by example. The sense of superiority was seductive.

But I was soon to learn, within three months of motherhood in fact, that we can be led into a false sense of security, especially if one's head is a little too far up one's arse! By the time Avalon was 12 weeks, she had taken to waking every hour and not sleeping in the day, making it near-impossible to work, clean the house or even think about saving the world. The torture of sleep deprivation left me reaching for cake and coffee, while swallowing humble pie!

As I formed close friendships in this time of baby survival, my judgments of other mums began to fade, to be replaced by a shameful realisation that those internal thoughts about people were of women simply doing their best and operating on their own values. I learned that life happens. If our intentions are good, then good is enough. There are worse things people could do than putting disposable nappies on their babies!

I discovered the real art of being the change I wished to see beyond ego, sharing from a place of compassion and non-judgment. And that began with not judging myself.

***

My little business was growing enough to make a few pennies here and there, but I spent most of my time trailblazing a whole new concept in a highly traditional funeral industry. At meetings with Avalon on my hip, funeral directors thought my company was sentimental and idealistic, but admired my energy and enthusiasm. I stuck out like a sore thumb at the trade shows, all smiles, laughter and friendly banter. I was one of a handful of females, clearly from another universe! Much to Harry's dissatisfaction, I would take our TV with me and display my photo montage videos of people's lives, which people watched in awe.

"You need to install a projector and a screen," I advised the local crematorium.

"Lou, I just can't see how investing that money will help people," the funeral director admitted.

"Trust me, Charles. Within the next 10 years, everyone will want a photo montage at their funeral."

I wasn't making much money, but I was creating waves in the industry. And I was right. People were looking for sentiment at their funerals.

***

CHAPTER 6

ME, YOU AND THE UNIVERSE

Magic of manifesting

"LOU, YOU CAN MAKE things happen with your thoughts," Nick said over the phone. "I've been thinking about you so much that I had to get in touch. You've gotta watch this DVD called *The Secret*. I know you'll love it. When I watched it, all I kept thinking was I had to tell you about this!"

I hadn't heard from Nick in ages. He'd been on various adventures: training to be a chiropractor, travelling the world, living a life of partying too hard even by my standards. I loved hearing his voice and the enlivening feel of the conversations we used to have back in that flat in London, a million miles from where I was now: trying to be a super-awesome earth-loving hippy mummy raising her baby to be kind, compassionate and strong, and running a business. I was so busy and so tired.

"I'm being a bit of a Poor Me, Nick. I'm so tired. I'm on the go 24/7. I'm fast becoming that martyr again. I keep blaming Harry. If he dares tell me he's tired, I bite his head off. I'm aware I'm doing it!" I laughed at myself as I told him, rolling my eyes. "I don't seem to have the mind control to snap the fuck out of it either, because I want to win the 'I'm more tired than you' game!"

"Lou, listen to me. You need to watch *The Secret*. It's all the stuff we used to talk about. You'll get it. You just have to change your belief system and know you deserve all that you want in your life. It's working for me already."

"Are you saying somewhere inside of my belief system I believe I don't deserve a moment's rest?!"

"No, just that you're creating this situation," Nick explained.

I felt defensiveness rising.

"I can't bloody help the fact my toddler wakes every hour and a half, and I think I'm going mad in the middle of the night!"

He ignored my moaning, "Lou, just get it, okay? It will change your life."

I fobbed him off, mumbling that I'd download it. At £30, I didn't really have the cash, plus I wasn't sure about this whole 'think of something and it turns up' concept. If it was so easy, why wasn't everyone a millionaire?

Two weeks later, Nick called back.

"Did you watch it?"

I admitted I hadn't, because we were broke again, but he insisted I find the video. Later that week, I saw the book in the window of a bookshop. I bought it and read it quicker than any book I had ever read. It filled me with hope, reminding me that my dreams of owning a big property with a swimming pool, a nice car, having financial freedom and running a successful business that would help millions of people in positive ways could come true, if I just believed them. *The Secret* taught something called the Law of Attraction, how our thoughts attract things, how to trust in the Universe, how to 'ask, believe, receive.' A lifeline of hope was thrown at me and it sparked a want for my business to become hugely successful, so we could buy fast cars and fancy houses, and live happily ever after.

I became a committed student for the first time in my life. For hours every night, I would read and take notes on the Law of Attraction. *Ask for what I want. Believe it's coming. Receive my manifestation.* I created vision books, wrote out plans, goals and dreams, and put it out to the Universe. The book said to start small, so I asked for a big house with a pool! Because I didn't really understand the concept of starting small!

It was inspiring to be positive about the world again and believe that anything could happen. Just in changing my mind from being tired and run down to being grateful and joyful at what the future held, I got back to being super mum, party mum, hippy mum, festival mum, personal development mum, business mum. I was nailing it. Things weren't perfect, but I was hopeful and focused on this manifesting thing.

Sure enough, within a few months I manifested a Mercedes. *Holy shit! What?* Only five years earlier, I had mentioned I wanted an LPG auto gas silver Mercedes 4x4. One day, my friend dropped round on her way to Dubai for a year and asked me to sell it. There were so few in the country that it made me pay attention. I knew this was my first manifestation. *Okay Universe, I'm listening. There's something in this!*

Buying that car boosted my ego no end. I had made the impossible possible. Behind that wheel, I felt successful. *Next stop mansion house with a swimming pool. Easy!*

***

Awakening the divine feminine

Turning 30 woke the goddess in me.

"I'm just really fucking horny all the time," I told my friends. "What is that?"

"They don't call it the Dirty Thirties for nothing," my best friend Sandy laughed.

"But it's not just sexual energy. It's something more."

I had a sense of confidence within, a fire inside that I had never encountered, and more power in my mind, body and spirit as my self-assurance grew. I believed in the strength and beauty of my body, and that soulful sexual connection was taking on a playful level. I was loving my body and it was loving me right back. My skin shone. My baby weight had gone — finally! — after two years. I had an awesome attitude again, and believed it could get even better. My thirties were rocking with a newfound faith. The goddess stirred. I was here for something more.

Practicing the Law of Attraction, I knew there was an energy I could tap into that I hadn't quite mastered, but that power came through sexually. Intimate connection was a sacred bond within my relationship with Harry — always had been. I was deeply protective of what we had grown. No plastic, no porn. We'd been there, got the t-shirt in our early twenties, and saw how it took us away from our own magic. Friends joked about my vanilla views, but I wanted a world for my children where they didn't get lost in their minds. When the time came, men would make love to them and connect with their souls, not bend them over, thinking about some 17-year-old performing a sex act in the videos they watched.

The world was changing. The internet was bringing about something I had no desire to be a part of. I saw it like a black shadow seeping into people's minds. In my world, sex was sacred. My hippy heart needed presence, mind to mind, heart to heart, soul to soul. I loved to feel waves roll between our bodies, bringing us higher and higher, closer and closer. It was something we had grown and nurtured. Over the years, we'd learned so much about each other's needs and what they meant. Sexual connection is a fragile balance, one that can take you in many directions. I was always discerning in where it took us — holding out for soul-shaking orgasms that held us united and came from deep in my belly, not from my mind, and not instant gratification from images of someone else's experiences.

Harry knew my body better than I did. He took me on journeys out of my body to worlds where colours and swirling energy wrapped around me. We breathed in unison. We travelled together towards powerful orgasms that would meet simultaneously and ripple through us.

I could see that manifesting and sex were sort of the same; both the power of creation, focused attention and love. I had a hunch that sex was part of manifestation. The more we made love, the more love we created in our life.

And now there was a new level because I was truly in love with my body. It wasn't what would be deemed *perfect*. I ate chocolate and never went to the gym. But I enjoyed my body and Harry always adored it. I was a peacock, displaying a glory of feathers, commanding and confident. And he would honour the beauty and meet me there. He was looking at me in a new way lately, like his goddess, and would tell me how incredible I was, or stop and watch me as I moved.

Turning 30 was not about sexual energy alone either. It was about all the energy around me.

"I can feel something inside. So much of me is desperate to fly, but I don't have wings. I have to go in search of some," I told Sandy. "I love life. You know that more than anyone. But I still have those fears I'm going to die in the blink of an eye. If it wasn't for the fact you would rally round Avalon, I would go insane."

"Oh don't, Lou. You need to stop talking like that or you'll manifest it," Sandy said.

Yes, Sandy was on board with the manifesting too. She loved me so much and always wanted the best for me. And she wasn't afraid to tell me when my thoughts and actions were out of line with my soul.

***

When the student is ready, the teacher will come

The train journey into London was liberating. It had been a long time since I had been on my own without a toddler needed my attention or work to do. I soaked in all of the freedom, tears in my eyes, pushing away the guilt that rose from my belly. *It's okay to be doing this. I deserve this. It's going to help me and Harry get what we need. I'm doing it for him, for me, for us.*

I had known from the start he wouldn't like it, me leaving him with Avalon all day, while I went off and did something for me, but I had framed it so he couldn't say no. "I don't want anything for my 30th from you, no gift, nothing, except a day to myself. Sarah told me about a Buddhist monk who teaches the natural law of attraction meditation. He's going to show me how to teach meditation. I've saved the money myself. You don't even have to cover the costs. I just need you to cover the childcare."

He agreed reluctantly, but I could feel his resistance. He'd never solo-parented before, we did everything together, but he also didn't appreciate me buggering off for the day for something he couldn't reconcile in his scientific mind. Often, he would take the piss out of my hippy ways, but I *had* to do this. Something powerful was guiding me to this day and I could not ignore it.

The robed man with beautiful blue eyes told me he was 70 years old, though he looked no more than 50. Sadhu was gentle in his energy, a contrast to my excitement, which was overcompensating for how intimidated I was by his quietness.

"There is a lot to learn about the Law of Attraction. Books like *The Secret* can bring distraction and trouble to people, because they do not focus on the real essence nor honour the power of this gift. First you must learn to master your mind through meditation so you have control of what you want to create. If you are not meditating you will be creating so much that is not in line with yourself."

The Secret teaches people to sit and trust that a brand new car, for example, will come to them just by thinking. That is not how the Law of Attraction works. That way of thinking traps people with illusions that don't serve them.

In many ways, it had done that to me. In other ways, it had awoken me to the magical creative force around us that we can tap.

My teacher talked and talked, and I didn't fully understand what he was saying. I could, however, see it in my own way: here we are with a key to a sacred garden, but the access to the garden is through the most tempting sweet shop, so we just keep finding ourselves with sweets that please us superficially and temporarily, but that we don't truly want or need. And we just stay there in the sweet shop and forget about the garden. The sweet shop distracts us from something greater. If we walked through that sweet shop, right to the end, we would find the doorway into the sacred garden where infinite abundance and wonder lie, our soul's true purpose. So far as I could tell, few people in this world were strong enough in themselves to get to the back of the sweet shop. For the first time in my life, I knew — just *knew* — that I was. I had the focus and drive to find my way into the sacred garden that would provide all I needed when I truly needed it. I had no idea how long it was going to take to learn how to walk past all the sweets, but one day I would get there.

Sadhu told me that his work as a monk was to understand all religion, so for 30 years, he had studied and found deepest affinity with Hinduism and Buddhism, becoming ordained in both. The meditation he had developed was based on Hindu, Buddhist and Jewish principles.

"I made friends from all different faiths and found the lines were so fine that I had to respect all those religions. Hindu and Buddhist teachers supported me in becoming ordained. I see no division in people and religions."

I loved this man right away. My heart opened as he spoke.

"This is how I felt the world too," I whispered, "As one." Our time together was filled with breathwork, pranic healing, learning to slow my breath. It was something I had always struggled with, but by breathing gently, I felt a shift. I marvelled at the simplicity.

The day took me deeper and deeper into stillness. And the monk broke down a complex meditation, teaching me stillness, embodiment, visualisations, chants. By the end of the afternoon, my whole body was vibrating. It was a stillness of mind I had never experienced before. I was fascinated by the warmth in my hands and Sadhu taught me how to use *this* energy to heal other people.

To create what you want, I saw that we have to be open to giving back the equal amount of energy in one form or another. It's more than just wishing. It's about knowing it on all levels and knowing yourself on all levels. We have to be in alignment. We can't just sit there hoping money will come, if we're not aligned with what we want. We work with the Universe. I could understand that now. We co-create and that's a dance along a path of knowing yourself so you can see what you're attracting.

Over the course of my day with Sadhu, I realised the contemporary teachings of the Law of Attraction missed some fundamental principles around being in union with the Universe, connection, compassion and spirituality.

"This chair you sit on is made of energy," Sadhu told me, "You must learn to have as much compassion for this chair as you do for the people in your life. Feeling that is knowing oneness and knowing your mind. Meditating to control your mind teaches you focus and helps you not have scattered thoughts."

As Sadhu spoke, he breathed so slowly that my own breath began to match his. I dropped into my belly and felt what he was saying to be true, even though my mind boggled. But wasn't that the point?

"All you need to do is commit to meditating every day. There is no excuse. You don't need crystals and candles. Just sit down every day and meditate for 20 minutes in the morning and 20 minutes at night. Make sure you have an empty stomach so that your body can rest. Your commitment will pay off greatly. You will align with the Universe and know the God within you. Morning and night, begin to feel compassion for all things, even the chair you're sitting on."

His words changed the way I felt, and his energy allowed me to feel that love, that compassion, even for the chair.

By the end of our time together, we'd put the whole meditation together, breathing, embodying, feeling compassion for all beings, then sending out the one intention I wanted for the world. It surprised me that what I wanted wasn't money...

"I want to feel like I'm here for a purpose. I want to know I am giving as much as I can to the world."

Sadhu nodded.

As we parted, he told me, "It's important you share this work."

I went home that evening knowing I had changed. I had something to commit to and wanted to shift from where I was. Over the weeks, I was surprised how this commitment changed me. I began to wake up at 5.30am before Avalon woke and sat for 20 minutes. Evenings, I was conscious that

I didn't want to have a full stomach, so would eat our family dinner at 5.30pm when Harry got home. After I'd put Avalon to bed, I would meditate for another 20 minutes, sometimes on my bed, sometimes in my office. No matter where I was, I would commit to it. Some days, it was so hard. All I wanted to do was move and twitch and look at the clock. I willed it to be over. But then I began to feel the effects and would find the time passed quickly. I would feel the light pouring over me.

Finding compassion for a chair was the real challenge! I could connect to everything that was living and breathing, but to a chair, to walls? How do you even begin to feel compassion for something inanimate? I found it hard enough to have compassion for people who had hurt me, let alone furniture. I thought about my own father who was once again not in my life, in his usual on-off way that depended on his latest girlfriend. I felt compassion towards him and words of healing and forgiveness came from the divine.

Everything is alive, Lou. Everything is made from the same energy in different forms. You must learn to feel that compassion for all people and all things, and send that out to the Universe.

And I let go of my anger towards him.

***

Tides begin to turn!

Every so often, tiny miracles happen in succession that will just about hold your faith in manifesting, gentle reminders that the Universe wants to play with you and that everything you need is right here if you dare to take a few chances.

The year 2009 had been a year of getting back to me. I was thoroughly enjoying being a mummy and getting my life back from the early baby stage. On occasions, Harry and I could ask the grandparents to babysit so we could have a night out. I was loving the return of freedom. I had always taken Avalon to parties and festivals. She was with me all the time and slept soundly in her buggy or upstairs despite the pumping sound systems. But I was never fully off-duty and had been craving the party lifestyle I'd had before I became a parent.

One night at a house party, our best friend Mark approached me and asked out of nowhere, "So when you going to have another baby, Lou?"

It was the last question I ever expected to come out of his mouth and it took me by total surprise. None of our friends had kids. Many were still off traveling the world, often moving into our house for months on end to save money to go off again. We lived vicariously through their travels and double-income-no-kids freedom. In some ways, I still felt I wasn't ready to have the first kid, let alone think about another!

I laughed off Mark's comment and listed all the excuses why I couldn't have another... AKA told him how many parties we had in the pipeline. Mark looked at me serious-faced and said, "There is always going to be another party, Lou. Avalon needs a brother or sister." And then walked off!

He'd never said anything like this to me before, and while I felt much love and care from him, it was as if he had channelled a message from the Universe that I didn't yet want to hear.

Next morning, lounging around in our PJs, recovering and eating crisps for breakfast, taking turns to make coffee and enjoying Avalon's abundance of aunts and uncles playing with her, I quizzed Mark, "Hey, what got into you last night lecturing me about having more babies?"

He had no recollection of our conversation!

"I must have been wasted!" he replied.

All the same, it had set a powerful seed. I looked back on my vision boards and saw a picture of me with a bump. Next to it were the words, "Pregnant at 31 and a half!"

Within two months, I felt the familiar feeling within my body and knew it was happening. Rock hard boobs, nausea coming thick and fast... I was pregnant again.

***

There is magic in the creation

I sat there counting the dates over and over as I flicked from page to page through my diary. There was no mistaking it. This baby was due over Glastonbury Festival weekend. *There's no other option. We can't miss the festival. We'll just have to have the baby there*, I mused. *It's meant to be.*

"We're gonna have to have the baby at Glasto. It'll be fine. There are loads of midwives and doctors on site," I declared to Harry, not giving him an inch to contest the idea. "No-one can deny the Universe wants us at Glasto. It has been in our blood for 10 years now. We live for that festival every year. It was the theme of our wedding. It was our honeymoon. We named our first child after it. We didn't let our first baby stop us from going and now it will be the birthplace of our second child. It's fate and it's fucking cool."

"It's a stupid idea, Lou."

"I'll just give birth in The Green Fields. It'll be fine."

Harry chose to ignore my ideas hoping that they would go away. And I chose to ignore his ignorance, smitten with the romance of the dreamiest birth at the greatest place in the world.

***

My meditation practice was slipping. I was four months pregnant and more exhausted than ever. I just wanted to sleep, but never gave myself permission to relax. It was the curse of 'being busy' that so many of us Western women carry. Somewhere in my belief system I thought being busy equalled 'being successful', and that if life wasn't busy, I couldn't be working hard enough. I was on the go from morning until night, but something had to change. I had to get back to where I had been when I was meditating. The stillness had gone. And I wanted it back.

Not many weeks after I had this thought, an email came through from a meditation retreat I had applied to go on the year before. They were offering a place the following weekend. I couldn't believe it! It was just what I needed.

"Babe, I need to go on this retreat. They finally have a space for me. Can I go? It's only two nights. I'll be back Sunday afternoon. And it's by donation so it won't cost too much."

I realised I was crying, utterly exhausted from the nausea. Still, I felt his resistant energy. We never had nights away from each other willingly, only a handful of times when he was away for work.

"I have so much work on, Lou. I've got to get these websites out the way."

He was head down building websites on top of his day job for extra cash. He was over delivering and under charging and losing patches of hair with stress. I knew it was bad timing and he hated being away from me. But this was the only opportunity before the baby was born. I had to take it.

"I know, babe, I know. But it's going to be the only time I will get for myself and I need to do this for me. Please. I never ask for any time, but I just have to go."

He couldn't say no to me and I knew I had to put myself first before I broke.

***

Getting back to me

I floated in and out of the grand halls of a beautiful stately home, dipping into meditation workshops, writing in my journal, wandering the gardens, immersing myself in the love, the energy and the silence that touched my soul.

I found a swing hanging off the tallest redwood I had ever seen. As I pushed myself off, the most wonderful exhilarating feeling washed over me. *I am so alive.* How had I become so busy that I'd forgotten my aliveness? As I flew through the air higher and higher, I laughed and sang like a child, going up, up, up into the unity, just me and my baby playing with innocent and infinite possibilities all around. *God, thank you, thank you, thank you.*

Lighter after my walk, I sat with 100 other people looking into the third eye of a yogi who was on the stage in front of us. We were meditating with our eyes open. For me, the whole room went white, her face changed, energy rushed up and down my body and I melted into the chair. Something was happening inside me again: peace, stillness, wonder, magic, aliveness. Another level. The yogi was blessing me and I was becoming one with her, with this baby, with the whole world. I felt like I was going to take off into the sky. It was better than any drug I'd ever taken. I was slipping through the dimensions. I was all and everything and nothing...

As the meditation ended, I got up and ran out. I couldn't take the intense energy that had filled my body, so I rushed to my room. And I sobbed and sobbed and sobbed, overwhelmed by what had happened. Now I knew. I knew what Sadhu had been teaching me; that compassion for all things was me. I was it. It was me. It was beautiful beyond anything I had ever known. It was oneness.

I explained what I had seen to the other residents and asked if they'd felt or seen what I had. They hadn't had the same experience. I felt their disappointment, so to take away that feeling I reassured them it was probably just because I was pregnant.

But I knew... I had had this experience because I had been asking for this awakening for a long, long time.

***

The energy makes itself known

I lay propped up on the massage bench, my big belly blocking my view of Alison's head as she worked on my feet.

"You're running at a thousand miles an hour, Lou. You need to slow down and rest."

"Yeah, I know," I said, more to appease her than anything, knowing full well this *was* my rest and I would have to get right back to it straight after.

I felt too guilty to stop. The need to be successful was not the only fuel; I had grown my business well enough to know that what I did was making a huge difference to people. I was like a grief healer and the work I was doing was helping heal the pain of those suffering the loss of their partners, children, parents, best friends through celebrating life. And I was good at it. I wanted my business to go national and I had one of the biggest corporate funeral firms interested in my company. I had to get back to work after this!

"Do you want a bit of Reiki?" Alison had a cheeky smile on her face as she asked me, like a white witch knowing what I needed.

"I don't really understand what it is. Think my friend did some on me years ago, but I don't really remember. I was so hungover. Give me whatever you have!"

I trusted her completely and was open to any renewal I could get in my hour-long session.

"Just relax," she spoke softly, "And close your eyes. Let everything go for now."

Her voice was the authoritative calm I was craving. I needed permission from someone I respected to switch off. The only other person who could give me that was Harry, but he was unaware of my need for permission, blinded by my drive and unstable bounces of energy.

I closed my eyes for a moment, as she cradled my feet, and let go of all I had to do that afternoon. I surrendered to the gentleness of her hands. Involuntarily, a huge breath rose up through my body and left with a big sigh. I drifted into a place where I was free of all thought, but then felt pinned down to the bench. The most intense feeling, a huge fireball of light energy shot up through my feet, up my legs into my belly, and exploded power into me, filling every part of me. The baby kicked like crazy. Before I had time to process what had happened, I sat bolt upright and words fell out of my mouth, "Whatever that was, teach me how to do it."

Alison looked up with as much surprise, "Wow! Did you feel that?"

"Yes, I felt that! What was it? That was insane. I mean it. You have to teach me how to do it!"

Alison laughed.

"Well, I've done my Reiki Masters, so I suppose I could, but I've never taught anyone before."

I didn't care. I looked at her, willing her to understand that I needed to know what it was. That energy was power, beauty, something I had never known yet understood deeply.

It was part of who I was.

***

Manifesting 'that car'

Cars seemed to represent so much more for me than they did for other people. Growing up, all my parents' friends had Bentleys and Astons outside their big houses, and I always felt a deep sense of inadequacy. Not having a nice car made me feel unworthy or unsuccessful.

The Mercedes we had manifested was far from trouble-free. Every month, something would go wrong with it and the repairs would cost us so much money. We needed a new car, but we were still living hand-to-mouth, and the Mercedes was now worth a fraction of what we had paid for it, so selling it wasn't a solution.

If the Law of Attraction was anything to go by, we had to stop focusing on what was wrong and look at what we wanted. We had to 'ask, believe, receive.' Yet I was still in doubt as to how we were ever going to buy a vehicle before our fast-approaching new arrival got here. For months, we played Let's Pretend, a 'dare to dream' sort of game that I had learned to allow myself. There were no limitations to pretending.

What if money wasn't an issue? What would we choose then? I asked myself.

The trick to the game was to not be so far out that it was unbelievable. It had to be enough of a stretch to feel like a dream, but close enough that it could become a reality if we worked hard at manifesting.

Harry wanted a BMW X5. That seemed beyond what was possible in my mind, but his interest in the Law of Attraction was piqued, now that it involved cars. Anything else and it was 'bullshit hocus pocus', but all of a sudden he seemed willing to play.

"How much do you want to spend, Lou?" Harry asked playfully.

I plucked a number out of the air, "Let's say £20k."

"Here's one two miles away," Harry said.

We called the garage feeling naughty and out of our depth, like frauds. We couldn't even afford next week's shop, or a clapped-out old banger, let alone a nice BMW. But we were up for the game. I put on some makeup and my best clothes, which were limited during my pregnancy and a bit tatty even at the best of times, and we set out to see the blue BMW.

Surprised by my air of detachment, I found that the car didn't impress me much at all.

"In all honesty, Harry, I wouldn't pay £20k for this car even if I had it," I told him as I looked around the car's basic interior. It felt almost soulless. I tried the sound system and was hugely disappointed. I drove it unimpressed; it's just a car.

"Well, that's what you get for £20k!" Harry said, frustrated with me. "What were you expecting?"

I could tell some part of him believed we could have this car. We left the garage and the car behind, but playing the game had started to take hold. We were talking like this was an actual possibility, like we had £20k to spend on a car, even though our circumstances hadn't changed. We tried another place.

"I want blacked-out windows and leather heated seats. I want a badass sound system and bigger wheels. And I want it in black."

"You're looking at £30k for a car like that, mate."

"Well, I don't want to spend more than... £19k?"

"It's not going to be possible, I'm afraid."

We went home.

Undeterred, Harry sent me links to X5 ads from the internet. I kept denying them as if I was a rich lady of the manor unimpressed with the riff-raff he was sending me!

"Not enough spec on any of them, babe. Sorry."

Then I found an image I liked and sent it to him. Indeed, it was a black X5 with silver runners, blacked-out windows, cream leather interior, a badass sound system and even a ski bag! It was way out of my league, but it looked sexy. And for a moment, I let myself dream of having a car just like that. After I'd messaged Harry, I printed it off and stuck it on my ever-growing manifesting wall above my desk, full of images of everything I wanted to be, do and have.

"That's £29k, Lou!" Harry emailed back.

"I know. But I want that car for £19k and with a two-year warranty," I wrote back flippantly, playfully and incredibly detached. I was enjoying playing the game with him.

"In your dreams, Lou!"

The following weekend, I was due to do a 5k race around Hampstead Heath. I was eight and a half months pregnant and had taken on the challenge to prove a point: that pregnancy didn't stop me. Just as we left the house, we noticed a BMW dealership leaflet had been posted through our door with a headline: "Two-year warranties on all second-hand BMWs this month!" Harry picked it up as we were rushing out.

"Look at that," he laughed. "It's a sign!"

It wasn't even our local BMW dealership, but one about 15 miles from our house. It was strange to see it in the post, but I didn't take much notice. I laughed, but I was over the BMW thing, and immersed in baby mode.

I had to run this race without baby coming early, then plans for having this baby at Glastonbury might even come true. (Our crew camping passes had arrived for the green fields and the medics had been emailing me: they knew I was coming, but I had instructions to leave the site right away if I went into labour!) I fast-walked most of the race but kept an amazing pace with one of my best friends who just laughed at me all the way. I ran the last kilometre and could hear Avalon screaming, "Go, Mummy!" which spurred me on. I felt how proud she was, how proud Harry was, and I was proud of myself too. I looked ridiculous crossing the finish line – red, puffy-faced, huge belly – but I'd been determined to do it and I'd done it. That baby sure felt a lot lower than it had been before though!

We headed back in the car, the mid-summer heat making me sweat. As we began to drive through London, the car spluttered and died! It had overheated and there was no water in the tank again. Harry got some water and filled it up, but it poured straight out the other end. Clearly, there was a leak.

"Fuck, we need to get her working," I worried, glancing at the traffic building up around us. We were causing an obstruction. "There's no way we can sell her on now," I added, "She is officially fucked. It would be bad karma to pass her on to anyone."

"But there was a clear sign this morning," Harry protested.

"It certainly does look like the Universe wants us to get rid of this car and get a BMW," I laughed, considering our broken heap.

"Let's get it working and go part-exchange her at BMW. There isn't any other choice. We'll go to the place where they're doing the two-year warranties," Harry decided.

It was agreed. He got the car working, filled the tank, and we crossed all our fingers and toes as we drove the 25 miles to the dealership, somewhat certain the Universe had plans for us and that we just had to trust. Even though the car was buggered, I knew it was going to make it.

We pulled in, and there on the forecourt, with no signs on it, was a badass black BMW X5 just like the one in the picture I had sent Harry. Our energy was different today. There was no need to pretend we were rich or blag that we could afford a new car.

"What's that X5 out there?" I asked the salesman straight up.

"It's only just come in this morning, I'm afraid. It hasn't even been cleaned and there are no signs on it, so I'm not sure how much it's being sold for," he said.

The second he said it had only just come in, I knew that car had come in for us. All the threads had led us to this place.

"That's the car," I said to Harry. I turned back to the salesman, "Can you find out how much it's going on the market for, while we take it for a drive, please?"

He went to check and came back, "My colleague thinks it'll go on at £19,950, but it's not even on the system yet, so I'll have to wait to take it for a drive."

I laughed – *of course!* – knowing that somehow this car was going to be ours. I got in and felt the cream leather seats, took in the walnut dash. It even had the chrome, the blacked-out windows and the ski bag...

"Mummy, I want this car," Avalon said.

"Me too, baby girl. I think we'll call her Black Betty."

I turned up the sound system. It sounded amazing. Everything was amazing. I was so in love. This car was for me...

I'm not sure how, but within the hour, we'd bought the car for £19,000 on finance. I had raided my business bank account that had some savings in there for marketing, Harry had raided his business bank account and discovered he'd been paid for a website he'd just built, and we had worked out a finance plan that stretched us, but still felt doable. We'd find a way to pay the £250 every month.

Amazingly, we always managed it, because from the moment we bought the car, we felt that much more abundant and didn't even notice the extra money coming out each month.

As we drove off the forecourt, Harry looked at me and said, "Well done, babe. I don't know how you did that, but even I'm going to thank the Universe today."

***

The Universe has its own plans

I screamed in pain, looking up to what seemed like a hundred faces, running alongside my hospital bed so fast the lights flashed by like a strobe down the corridor.

"The baby is in distress, there's no heartbeat."

Doctors, nurses, surgeons appeared from nowhere. I wanted to die. I didn't care anymore. I just wanted the pain to stop. This was not what I had spent the last nine months envisioning. None of them could see me. They saw a body, a situation. I needed someone to see me.

As the theatre doors opened, increasingly serious faces appeared above me, detached from me, focused on the job. No one was listening to me. No one could hear my cry. No one would hold my pleading hand. *Please, someone see me, someone hold me.* I was the job. A life they had to save. No time for comfort.

God must have heard my cries and sent an angel down. Right there and then, through the bright theatre lights, a face amongst all the other faces appeared. Her hand reached down towards me, locking on tight to my own, her warm gaze met mine. Without words, she reassured me that everything was going to be all right. I had no sound left in me. I couldn't even scream. All I could do was hold onto her. I was no longer alone.

The spinal block crept up my body like a warm duvet of comfort and peace. I took a breath. It felt like I hadn't breathed for a lifetime. Life was coming back to me and a life was coming out of me. Beyond the blue screen, my baby was coming. I knew she was alive. It was a 'her.' I knew it deep inside me. I could feel her, and I already loved her with all my heart. The rising love for her choked me and tears slid down the side of my face.

And then the tension in the room dissipated. A scream. She was alive. I was alive. *Bella, my beautiful baby girl. Bella, I love you, I love you, I love you.*

And my next thought was, *How the hell am I going to get to Glastonbury now? We'll get there. It'll be fine. A lot can happen in four days when you put your mind to it!*

***

"You okay, Lou?" Sandy asked, as my tears fell.

"I'm just watching this moment," I said dreamily.

I was in heaven. *I'm actually here, back home on the lands of Glastonbury Festival in the Healing Field!* It was a dream I could never have created in my mind.

We sat under a bright parachute canopy, watching the way the multi-colours danced in the welcome breeze. I watched people as they entered the miniature healing gardens, eyes wide open like they had just fallen down Alice in Wonderland's rabbit hole. They came through the wicker arches and passed peace emblems hanging between the tents and yurts of the mystics and crystal healers. Music drifted in from a wandering choir, all dressed in floaty white robes singing 'give peace a chance' with drums and bells and circling flags. The sky was electric blue and quite surreal. Our friends surrounded us, eating ice cream and drinking beer, as we relaxed in the shade. Avalon danced around in her long loose dress, twirling like an angel to the songs playing next to us. The beats matched my heart and soundtracked this sacred moment. And here, snuggled against my breast, was my five-day-old little doll.

"I have brought you home, baby girl. This is who you are and you are here for something big. I can feel it."

For five days, I walked the fields, slept on the grounds, and wandered from tent to tent, stage to stage, stall to stall, sacred healing space to sacred healing space, rave to rave. I didn't look like I'd just had a major operation five days before. The lands were carrying me. They were healing me. And I was bringing my daughter home to begin her new life here on earth.

I knew I was walking these girls down a different path to the one that dictates and constrains our society. And I was watching my husband surrender a little each time to my wild ways.

***

Awakening the lightworker

I had waited two months since the day Alison sent a fireball of Reiki into my belly. Finally, she was about to teach me how to connect to the power of Reiki through my first attunement and I was hungry, open, ready and more than willing to know more.

I closed my eyes, feeling the stillness wash over me as she placed her hands on my shoulders. I felt safe and secure with Alison. She knew me well. She knew how to calm and ground my high energy. I relaxed deeply. Even with my eyes closed, it felt as if someone had turned a light on in the room. Before I had time to figure it out, the light entered my body. As I raised my hands, bolts of lightning went through me. I saw images, so many images. I couldn't grab them to see what they were. There were castles and coloured lights — red, white, purple, green — all around. I was back there... *euphoria*.

When she finished, I was crying, and Alison was taken aback.

"Thank you, thank you, thank you. That was amazing! I could see colours and images and light."

"Do you want to come and have a go now?" she asked.

"Yes! But what do I do?"

Alison lay on the massage bench. All of a sudden, this mother archetype I looked up to as a powerful woman was expecting me to do something.

"Just put your hands around my head and see what you can feel," she suggested.

Oh my God! I could feel something. I could feel her energy and I could feel energy flowing out of my hands. It was so fast it was insane.

"Wow! This is magical. *This* is what I've been waiting for."

I ran my hands about two inches from her head. Her eyes opened and looked up.

"That's enough for now. It's too strong for me."

She shook her head and I looked on in awe. She didn't like me doing this to her because it was too much, but I took that as a good sign!

"Go home and practice. Do Reiki on yourself every day and you will learn to use it well."

"That's it?"

Alison nodded, "You can do your Reiki 2 when you feel ready. You'll learn more then, but for now, you just need to go and do Reiki on yourself."

I made it my mission. For months, I swung between, "Is anything even happening?" to "Oh my God!!" Some days I could feel it, other days I couldn't. But every day I tried.

I placed my hands on my body and got a tingle here and there. I was committed to seeking those highs I'd experienced the first time.

***

Reiki worked. I proved it to Harry by making him lie down naked on the bed while I hovered my hands about five inches away from his balls. After a few moments, his eyes lit up.

"Okay, okay, Lou. I believe you. That's fucking weird!"

Reiki was opening me up. All of a sudden, I was full of positivity, excitement, energy and enthusiasm. It was like I had superpowers. As I did Reiki on myself, my faith in the unseen energies of the Universe became unwavering. I knew the only way I needed to live now was to keep growing the Reiki connection and seeking the patterns that would lead me to create my dream life.

This energy rubbed off on Harry. His need for safety and security shifted to a desire to be together as a family. He had a new level of trust in me too. I was showing him that we could create visions in our mind and make them happen in our real life. He still didn't *quite* buy into it.

And yes, we still wanted to build a nice life for ourselves — the big house filled with friends and family, the parties every weekend, the swimming pool full of laughing kids. But there was something we realised we wanted more...

***

One giant step for change

"I miss you guys every day," Harry said from his offices in London the day he returned to work after two weeks' paternity leave.

"I want to stay at home with you and the girls. I don't want to miss out on any more time with you guys by being on the train into London, when I could build websites from home and see you all the time."

At night, my dreams were vivid. I could see us working together in an office with wooden windows leading out onto a street.

Sharing my dreams with Harry sparked off conversations and lofty ideals about quitting his job and having amazing businesses where we worked together. We were dreamers, we liked to fantasise about 'one day when we are rich' conversations but we never seemed to move far from the hand to mouth paradigms we were trapped in.

Harry's desperate want to leave work meant he was more open to the idea of manifesting and that meant I could talk more about my favourite subject — leaping and trusting the Universe will take care of the rest. It wasn't his usual style, but the Universe gave him a little nudge by our manifesting a car story and he had begun to accept there was something in this manifesting.

Two weeks later, Harry was offered a promotion at work. Instead, he quit his job.

"This could be the craziest thing we have ever done. I don't often feel brave, but you must be rubbing off on me Lou. I just somehow know everything will be okay," he said. "We may have to live on baked beans for a while, but let's do it!"

**

CHAPTER 7

WHERE OUR SUFFERING HIDES

Keeping faith in 'something'

"THERE IS SOMETHING about everything that you can be glad about, if you keep hunting long enough to find it," so Pollyanna said.

Yet, there is something about feeling and honouring our pain, going to those places where we hide our suffering, to alchemise that darkness into golden wonder. Because through pain, we grow into something greater than we have known.

Everyone was waiting for the world to end, because the Mayan calendar didn't go any further than 21 December 2012. The Western predictions were an apocalyptic hell, but the esoteric understanding was that the world *as we knew* it was ending. And 2012 was the first wave of energy awakening many of us to a new consciousness, which would change things for the future. This meant that the darkness was coming out to be seen, both in the world and in ourselves. The rumbling began. The cracks appeared. All so that the light could begin to seep in.

I didn't really know what true consciousness was, nor did I know this wave was the beginning of my own apocalypse. It was going to hurt yet it would present me with miracles that proved the world was not what I thought it to be. But there is no growth and no enlightenment without first going into the dark.

Life was about to turn upside down, to raise me high and take me low for a few years, so that I could land where I was meant to be, and not where I thought I should be.

***

I always saw the sunshine through the rain, thought happy thoughts so good things would happen, and didn't let life get me down. That was a superpower that stopped me from ever feeling desperately sad. I had such faith in the Universe that everything was going to turn out alright that it always did — just.

This approach meant there was only so far I could go. Unless I went backwards in time and unhooked the beliefs from the past that were holding me back, I could not move forward. And I wanted to move forward. Saying that is one thing. Doing it, actually going to those places, is quite another.

And how could I complain? I had manifested a family and a gang of awesome friends — tick! A cool little office in a funky little town that had come to me in a dream — tick! I could take Bella into work so no-one else had to look after her — tick! I had a nice car— tick! I had been on *BBC Breakfast* talking about my business to the whole nation — tick! I had a corporate client who was looking to grow my business to a whole new level — tick! I had my own radio show — tick! To top it all off, I was fast becoming well-known for my wisdom and strange-almost-psychic intuition, and well-respected as a Reiki healer, and a good one at that — double tick!

I was fully enchanted by the infinite possibilities of co-creating with the Universe, but deeply frustrated with the fact that I could not manifest financial security. I was hungry and yearning to feel a deeper purpose for being on the planet. All I had manifested sounded pretty impressive. I had made all these cool things happen, asking the Universe every day, playing make-believe, having a positive mental attitude, building vision books, being eternally grateful for everything, meditating and doing Reiki healing on my emotional blocks. I'd had faith to take giant leaps and do what scared me, like quitting jobs and rocking up to broadcast a radio programme with no previous experience! But we lived on the edge, I took risks, there was no security or safety and some days we had no idea how we were going to pay the rent. But somehow, we always just made it. Flying by the seat of our pants was normal, exciting even.

Even Harry, on days when it suited him, would surrender the science and agree that 'this manifesting thing' really did work. But we were still always broke! We could manifest everything but financial security.

My radio shows fed my ego. I found more courage to speak and share my thoughts about the Universe and mystic on Facebook All of a sudden, more people wanted to know me. Facebook friends increased by hundreds in a matter of months. I was on fire. And even though Bella didn't sleep most nights and I thought I was actually going insane from sleep deprivation, the fire in my belly was still roaring. I had new awareness, a deeper wisdom and a sharper intuition, accompanied by a profound need to help others feel the same aliveness I felt.

While this fire was roaring, I was going somewhere in my life. I became a white witch and confidante to so many people. I could see into their souls, and my words and Reiki healing took them to places they had not been before. I was everything to everyone and began to feel it was my purpose to save people from their pain and suffering. A lesson that every healer has to learn at some point is that this is not our pain to take; we are simply the space-holders, a conduit for the light.

Highs and lows in the school of enlightenment

But I was fast to learn that life is about balance. What goes up must come down. I was high on manifesting an outwardly 'successful' life, like a kid stuck in that sweet shop, but I was unravelling on the inside. Something — suppressed for a long time — was triggered by a succession of events and gradually life started to go wrong, which over the course of the year, would begin to show itself.

It started with our finances.

Harry was once again over-delivering in his work, which meant 16-hour days. The corporate company I had put all my hopes in to grow my business pulled out. Our dreams of getting out of a financial hole began to shatter. I kept plugging away at bits and pieces, but every job I did seemed to come with a whole host of issues. I was even beginning to resent my own home. The house looked so shabby, but because we didn't own it, we were stuck with threadbare carpets and damp. Nothing was flowing. It was like something didn't want me to do my businesses anymore.

Aside from finances, other events took their toll. I met a healer at an event, who had all these little bottles with different colours and smells. It stirred a memory, something dark from childhood that I couldn't understand. I brushed it off as being nothing and tucked that box away, but tiny invisible snakes started working their way into my soul. It would be another 18 months before my deepest wounds would fully show.

Then my dad went AWOL *again*! I had lost count of the times he'd slammed down the phone on me and disappeared out my life for years on end only to return as if nothing had happened. I never used to think it bothered me; I loved him and I knew he loved me. I had learned that his own suffering meant this was just the way it was. Rejection or guilt had been a normal pattern for us and I had become numb to it. It didn't hurt usually, but this time it did. It triggered something like a stabbing in the heart. Every day, I experienced feelings of insecurity and manic highs and big lows. Harry brushed off my ranting and bitching like an annoyance, not understanding why it was bothering me so much now, after happening for years. No-one liked a grumpy Lou, so I painted on a smile and took on the world, even though an inner unrest was telling me something wasn't right.

As the strange and transformational energy of 2012 crept into our lives, shadows lurked. My best friend Sandy had survived an attack the year before where she was randomly stabbed in a London park one snowy Monday morning, only moments after hanging up the phone to me.

This attack broke her inside and out. For a year, all I could do was allow the Reiki to flow. Healing her and letting the energy do its work on her was one of my biggest lessons in the power of Reiki. This trauma was too big for my mind, but we each had a knowing that the divine was at play; it was a journey that was teaching us both. I was there to help her heal. At the time, l had no idea how. Yet I was connected energetically to this experience of hers and the way it would play out in my own life 18 months later.

This healing power was growing inside of me and it was more than I knew was possible. Self-healing took me into worlds I had never seen. I simply closed my eyes and I would have visions of strange places and faces. It got stronger the more I believed and I knew it was limitless. I just needed to commit. I would lie in bed with one hand on my heart and one on my belly, feeling the light pour out of my palms. My entire body would light up, tingle, vibrate. I could follow the flow and see where it was getting stuck. My legs would twitch to help the energy move down to my feet.

"I can feel that, Lou," Harry said one night as he lay next to me, the energy pouring out of my body into his.

It had become part of my nighttime routine to place one hand on him and one on me, healing us both, sending us off into dream worlds where dragons played and angels came alive.

To go deeper into this energy, I knew I needed to find someone else who would do this with me. That's when Donna walked into my life. Fellow radio presenter, fellow miracles believer and the only person I knew who also knew Reiki! We would either go out and get drunk as hell together, which was something I was doing more and more lately to numb the constant fear of having no money or real purpose, or we would meet up weekly and do half an hour of Reiki on each other and go into these mad worlds where we both had huge visions. My fear of not having any money would be replaced by an awakened connection to my desire to live a bigger purpose. Around Donna, it was okay to not be happy all the time and to explore what was really going on inside.

One day, as I placed my hands on her, I saw her covered in angelic armour, indigo and purple. She was a fierce protector-warrior energy. As I closed my eyes, I saw visions of flowers. Then it was my turn, she put her hands on me and I drifted off into tranquillity and space. It was so beautiful to receive the energy that I gave to everyone else. Relaxing, I saw an angel falling through a stained-glass window above an altar. It was Archangel Gabriel and I knew this, even though I thought at the time that Gabriel was female, and this was a giant male light-being. I had never encountered an angel like this before. I lay there in wonder, eyes closed, feeling blessed.

Then I asked the angel, "What is my purpose here in the world?" and he replied, "Like sugar in everyone's life."

Is that it? my ego cried. The angel's light was bright and was telling me something more, but I couldn't hear it, even though I could feel it was important. The session was over. But I didn't want it to end. I wanted to stay there with Donna's hands on me forever.

Our weekly sessions took me to many more places. Over bridges. Through seas. Donna's visions were as strong as mine. She was acting as an earth angel guiding me to the next level. There was more to discover in this soul awakening; it was like I had all the ingredients for an epic meal that would feed thousands and be utterly delicious, but nothing to cook it in!

This pull of my purpose was now so strong it began to hurt.

***

Faith in Angels and Rainbows

I had assumed the path to wisdom was going to be joyful, happy, blessed, exciting, enlightening, but I was starting to feel frustrated. Yet whenever I lost faith in the angels, I would feel a pressure on my forehead like a halo, or a robin would pop up at the window, or a white feather would fall down from the sky, often into my hand as I was walking out the front door. A path of white feathers would appear if I asked for a sign and I would smile and whisper, "Thank you. I know you've got this."

In times like these, I would bounce into the house and tell Harry, who inevitably would roll his eyes and quip, "A bird gets massacred and you see it as a sign from the angels. Only you, Lou."

Sometimes the little signs were just enough to hold my faith when I had to leave the supermarket without my shopping because my card was declined. I could make all sorts of amazing creations appear, but could I get a penny in my bank account? Nope! That's when I needed to see some hope and asked the Universe for a rainbow.

"I need to know you're listening to me. I need to know you're hearing my call. Send me a rainbow. A real one. Not on my social media or on a passing car. I need a real live rainbow. I'm struggling. I'm losing faith."

When I felt like this I always went for a walk or run by the river. Exercise and nature was always a healer. I had a 'walk and talk' buddy who happened to be Harry's PA and a strong believer in the Universe and angels and all things woowoo! Emily and I would walk for miles by the river while Bella took her afternoon nap in the buggy.

We had connected due to a deep and profound vision I'd had while doing Reiki on her: a vision of an artist, a beautiful woman dying by striking white cliffs. She told me her mum was an artist and was going through chemo. Without telling her the full story of the death I'd seen, I described the vision and she relayed it to her mother who confirmed she had had the same one during her chemotherapy. I worked with her mother and had one of the most intense Reiki moments, knowing I was fully in service. The Reiki was so strong that I felt pain as if I had put my hand in a plug socket. In my mind, I was concerned I would hurt this delicate and frail woman, but my spirit guide whispered to me, *'You're not hurting her; you're helping her.'* She opened her eyes and locked with mine as I looked at her. I felt such love, because in that moment I knew she was going to die, and she knew I knew. We talked about the release and I never saw her again, but I was sure that day she was making sure her daughter would be okay and bonding us together.

I helped Emily through the grief of her mum passing. She taught me about the food I was eating and helped me curb my sugar addictions. And most of all, we would walk in nature, talking and discovering the world of manifesting together.

***

Emily saw my eyes flicking upward towards the sky and knew I was willing the clouds to come in and rain to fall, for a rainbow to happen on this dry sunny day.

"Stop looking for the bloody rainbow, Lou," Emily laughed, "There is so much fear it's not going to come that you're more likely to manifest doubt than a rainbow."

She was right. We were good at pulling each other up when we slipped into a negative destructive frame of mind. Nothing came of the rainbow, so I had to let it go. Disappointment faded into daily chores, school runs and after-school clubs. I found a fiver in the back of my purse, though, and thanked the Universe anyway.

It was 5pm when we got home. I unhooked Bella from her car seat, grabbed Avalon's school bags, and made to go inside. The sky was dark and evening was coming. I turned around and looked up to see a stunning rainbow, glowing brightly against the looming clouds. My stomach clenched in shock and the sensation rose into my chest, where I was still holding my breath. Avalon started shouting, "Rainbow! Rainbow!" and I released my tension and sobbed on the side of the road.

"Thank you, Universe, thank you, thank you."

Yes, it was unbelievable. This was what my life had become. I had faith that my dreams were going to manifest and I wanted relief from financial struggle and a nice home where all our friends could come with their kids every weekend to party, play, heal and hang out. Most importantly now though, I wanted to live a life of *purpose*. Whatever that was! I thought if I kept asking and believing, it would come. Yet, it never materialised.

There was so much more I had to learn first apparently. I had scratched the surface, seen there was a world beneath, an energy I could tap into, but there was still a whole universe to uncover.

***

I was like a yoyo. I had faith in the Universe, I was joyful and bright, I was happy and grateful. I woke up and gave thanks for every new day. I would dance and play with the kids and Harry, but deep inside, there was a part of me that was fed up of waiting for 'something' to happen, 'something' to change. A part of me that was constantly wondering, *What am I here for? What's my purpose on the earth? How can I help more people?* I felt like I was in a waiting room, being held back!

I was sabotaging myself with old habits: drinking and partying too much at weekends, smoking, avoiding domestic duties, going on Facebook too much. My week days were no longer spent in the office with Harry getting energised about my business. Bella was too noisy over there, so now I was working from home, missing Harry and hoping I could at least *try* to make my funeral business work during naptime.

In the evenings, I would go out and see Reiki clients. Sometimes my sessions went on for hours. I was over-delivering and sometimes not even charging. At least in healing, I felt I was doing something good. I found my worth in helping people. But I was on the go too much and running out of my own energy, often stuck down with migraines, which seemed to be the only time I took any rest at all.

Even by two years old, Bella wasn't sleeping at night, waking sometime five or six times. Then I would be up at the crack of dawn to do three (sometimes four) breakfast radio shows. At the time, I couldn't see that my frantic busyness was mirrored in Bella's sleep.

I didn't know what I was doing or where I was going. I could be full of the joys of spring on the outside, but deep inside, I felt like I'd failed my business and had no future plan. I sat scrolling on social media to avoid feeling lost, trying to find some importance in the moment. I checked my inbox for a change from Facebook.

Subject: Learn to Be a Conscious Awareness Coach

I ignored it. It was one of *those* emails from a networking site that I never opened. I got up to make another pot of coffee, which combined with my rekindled smoking habit was my main pleasure these days. It was another distraction taking over, but I was unwilling to contemplate giving up. It was my friend! As I flicked on the kettle, a sense on the inside nudged me. *Go back and read that email.*

So I did. It sounded interesting, but the training was up in London. *I can't head off and leave Harry with the kids. He does enough so that I can do the radio every day.* I left it and walked outside with my cup. I sat and rolled my cigarette, enjoying the ritual, then lit up and watched the clouds move across the sky. I looked around at the garden. It was a mess. The greenhouse had become a dumping ground for stuff we couldn't fit in the shed. The kids couldn't play out here because the steps and fence were falling down. It was a shithole.

As I smoked, a deep frustration gathered. *I fucking hate not being able to do anything to this house. I wish it was ours. I hate having to admit to people we don't even own it. Come on, Universe, make something happen. Or just send me a massive house. I'm bored of this place being such a dump. Show me what I need to do!*

I seemed to forget that this home was Harry's great-grandmother's. I reminded myself it had been chosen just for us and we were blessed to be paying cheap rent. I stubbed out my cigarette and went back inside. *Go back to that email,* my inner sense guided.

"Okay, I'm going, I'm going!"

I sat down and did as I was told. I read it to the end, "If you would like to know more, put your number in here and I'll call you back within 24 hours."

Fine, I'll do it. Nothing to lose!

My phone pinged an hour later with a text.

"Hi, this is Mikel. Can I call you this evening about 10pm to talk though the mentor coaching?"

I scoffed, *Who the fuck wants to talk at 10pm at night?*

"Dear Mikel, I will be meditating at that time, so I won't be available."

I paused and felt something. *Just say yes!* I deleted what I'd typed.

"Hi Mikel, yes, no problem."

***

The Mentor

Spring was in the air when I went into London to meet Mikel at a group coaching session he was holding. In his presence, I felt instantly like I had a wise big brother, the brother I had always wanted. Mikel talked about stuff I had no idea about, yet I could feel his energy like a Jedi! From the front of the room, he looked directly at me, our eyes locked, and something happened, a transmission of some kind.

There was a connection, an energy exchange, then everything began to go blurry, apart from his face. Everyone around us disappeared. It was just me and him at that table. I felt myself shift into another space, another dimension. I didn't understand what was happening but my forehead was pounding.

The room came back to me and everyone was gathering up their pens and papers to leave. As we wandered to the door, I thanked him for his time, then it just slipped out.

"Mikel, did you feel that in there, between us? Please know I'm not coming onto you or anything. It's not like that. I'm happily married. But there was something that happened. Do you know what it was?"

With surprise in his eyes, he said he had, "It was awesome, wasn't it?"

I asked if he'd felt a buzzing like it before, but he hadn't, so I told him about my experience with the yogi at the retreat a few years back.

"I'm a bit mind-blown, Mikel. You're a bit like Yoda, aren't you?"

"I've never been called that before!" he laughed.

"Well, now I name you my brother Yoda!"

He gave me a hug and I felt safe. His intentions were good and pure.

"See you next week for your first session."

***

"I live in utopia," I told him proudly in our first mentoring session. "I'm living the dream. I have everything I need. I can make things happen with the Universe. I've manifested cars, and jobs, and a radio show. I'm a healer and I change people's lives with my intuition and healing."

I was trying to impress him, but Yoda's energy unnerved me. He had an ability to fill the space with silence and I wasn't used to it.

"I've got a blessed attitude and that makes good things happen. I'm happy and positive all the time and that makes people feel good," I continued.

He looked right through me.

"That's your ego talking, Lou. You're not happy all the time!"

I was taken back by the directness of his response. I felt like a scolded little girl. How dare he question my positivity? I *was* happy! And wasn't that a good thing? I spent most of my days around people who were trying to get happy.

"Be truthful with yourself. Learning to become more consciously aware is being able to see deeper into what you hide from yourself."

He looked at me, compassion in his eyes, and I began to cry.

"But I am happy," I said defensively, wiping my tears. "There isn't anything *wrong* in my life apart from being skint all the time."

Yoda looked at me, almost like a knowing mother opening her arms into an embrace. His eyes showed me it was all going to be okay. *You're safe*, they said. Tears fell freely down my cheeks. I had no idea why I was crying.

"We're in so much debt. Any hope of buying a home of our own feels impossible. My business is crap. I seem to sabotage all opportunities for success. I can't charge clients money. I feel so bad because they are grieving and I feel guilty asking them for money. Often people come to me for healing and just walk out the door. I can't ask them to pay me. Sometimes we don't have enough money for food, but we drive a massive car and it takes nearly £500 a month in petrol, so it breaks us. But I like having a nice car because it makes me feel like I've made it and hides the shame that we have no money and that I'm a failure. I can see Harry feels like he's not a priority because I'm always on call to everyone else who needs me to heal them, fix them, rescue them. I'm everything to everyone else, so at weekends we just get trashed together and stay up all night. That's our 'thing.' It holds us together. But I get such horrific hangovers. It disconnects me from me. It makes me so ill that sometimes my head hurts so bad and I can't get out of bed for the next 24 hours, so we don't take the kids swimming, or do fun things with them. I hate myself for being a shit mum, choosing to party over doing things for them. I hate myself for smoking 20 cigarettes a day, eating too much sugar and crap. I look old in my skin because I abuse my body. I'm not doing enough exercise. My meditation is sporadic at best and I feel a conflict between my spirituality and my party girl. I'm up at the crack of dawn every day to do a radio show, then I try to run a business and solo-care for both my girls because I don't want anyone else raising them. And then a million and one people need me to do things for them. I don't watch TV because I hate TV and it makes me feel crap, but I would actually like the time to sit and watch some rubbish show once in a while. I don't stop, Yoda. And I'm fucking tired!"

I took a deep breath, surprised at the way I'd spewed my shame, looking at him for reassurance. He smiled.

"It's okay, Lou. I understand. What else is going on with you though? There's more."

It was like he could see through me, see into me, when he added, "You need to learn to stop."

"I can't stop. I don't have time to stop."

"But you're just building chaos on top of chaos. You've got no grounding. Have you heard that old story of the golden goose? She wanted to look after everyone in her life. She was everything to everyone. She would keep laying golden eggs to make those around her rich, but she never got looked after herself. All she did was give, give, give, then one day she became weak and died. You're the golden goose, Lou. It's time to look after you."

"But I do look after me," I said.

"It's time to slow down, learn to stop, look after yourself, nurture yourself, take time for yourself, so you can begin taking back control of your mind, so it stops distracting and destroying your body, your family and your life."

"But I have to do more for my kids. I can't stop looking after them. Plus, I need to make my business successful to earn money."

Yoda replied, "The way you're going, you'll end up like that golden goose — dead! — and then you'll be no good to anyone."

It sounded dramatic, but something was clicking for me. He was right about one thing. I couldn't carry on like this. I would burn out.

***

Everyone has issues!

I began to see Yoda every week for an hour of mentoring, which sometimes turned into two hours of him helping me to see myself beyond my ego. The aim was leaning into who I was inside, getting out of my head and into the present moment.

"All I want in life is to have a big house so all my friends can come over, a fleet of nice cars and a pool."

"Lou, that's your ego."

"It's my dream to see all my friends rock up every weekend and hundreds of kids playing in my pool. It's not ego," I insisted.

"Yes, it is. You want it, because you think it means success. You want success, because you've never felt successful, because deep down you feel unworthy. You think that you'll feel your worth, and therefore peace, by having a big house and business. The only thing is, in the weeks I've been mentoring you, I've questioned if you even know what the feeling of success is. Do you feel successful on the radio? You said, 'No, I'm a total fraud and I'm winging it.' Then I asked if you feel successful when you did events. You said, 'Nope, I just felt like it was a fluke that it all turned out perfectly.' What about your business? 'God, no. It's never taken off.' How about when you were earning money from your corporate clients? You said, 'No, it just feels like I wasn't really doing a lot of work for the money, so I felt bad.' Lou, can you imagine what success feels like?"

"Not really," I admitted.

"Then how are you ever going to manifest it?"

It hit me like a brick. Yoda went on.

"Why do you think you don't deserve to feel successful?"

"I suppose it's because I'm not clever."

Pangs of sadness washed over me. Yoda took a deep breath and held the stillness while I felt it. Silent tears of realisation and sadness for myself slid down my cheeks as I stared at my empty glass.

He gave me an assignment for the week. I was to do little things, like emptying the dishwasher or unloading the washing, and give myself some credit for it. I would spend the week awakening the feeling of success in the small things.

"You have to start from the beginning," he said.

So I did.

Sessions with Yoda went on for weeks and sometimes I didn't even have the money for them. He let me pay when I could. Each session went deeper. I would listen to him, barely understanding what he was teaching me, but knowing that it was shifting me.

If I talked to Harry about it though, I was met with resistance.

"That's just stuff I tell you, babe. Why do you have to pay someone money we don't have to tell you this stuff?"

But it wasn't *what* Yoda told me. It was deeper than that. I just couldn't explain it.

"Lou, you're gonna have to stop these sessions with Mikel," Harry sighed. "We just don't have any more money and I need you here to look after the kids. I'm struggling. I need to get on with my own work."

He was soft and gentle this time. I could see this wasn't coming from resistance, but from truth.

"Okay," I said, "Can I just go tomorrow and make it my last one?"

"Go tomorrow, but know we have nothing coming in and we're over our overdraft. I've got £100 cash you can have, but then we're cleared out."

I felt bad, really bad, but I had to go.

I met Yoda in London. After our one-to-one session, he was taking me to a group teaching at the coaching company he worked for. It was like walking into a sea of loveliness. *I've found my people!* Then suddenly I had a sinking feeling. *Shit, my car.* I was getting a ticket right that very second. I could feel it. I must have parked in the wrong bay. At the end of the training, I grabbed Yoda to come with me to the car. Sure enough, I had a ticket. *I bloody knew it.*

"Never mind, it's done now," I sighed, "No point getting upset about it."

Yoda looked at me.

"Lou, this is awful for you, because you don't have the money for it. You need to feel this."

"There's no point crying over it, dude," I said, as my inner Pollyanna came out, "Let's just go get a coffee before I need to go back. I've got an hour. No point paying again, seeing as I've already got a ticket."

As we walked along the streets of Chelsea, Yoda stressed the great lesson he saw.

"It's great to be positive, but you're missing a vital part. If you do not feel the pain and suffering of something bad, it will happen again and again. You need to feel this. When you've felt it, *then* you can find the silver lining." He paused as we walked, "Feel it, Lou. Feel how this will impact you and your family. Feel the sadness and the shame."

I couldn't though. I brushed it off and carried on walking. I could sense his disapproval. After lunch, I returned to the car, thinking I needed to make some money next week so I could carry on my sessions. And then I saw it... my car was clamped!

"Sorry love, it's £250, and we can't make it out to you for at least the next four hours."

"But I don't have £250!" I cried.

"Then we will impound it in four hours' time."

I sobbed and sobbed. I tried calling Yoda. I needed help, advice, something. His phone was off. And then I felt it, the shame, the sadness, the guilt, all that I had put Harry through. And now I couldn't even get back to take the kids so he could work. I had no choice. I had to call him. He didn't react.

"I have a company credit card with £300 left on it. You'll have to use that," he told me coldly.

In those four hours waiting for them to come take the clamp off the wheel, I sat underneath an old oak tree and poured out all my stuff. I wrote and wrote and wrote for hours, all the pain I had suppressed.

I got home at teatime. Harry didn't fall out with me. He just didn't want to talk to me.

And that was so much worse.

***

I was my own contradiction. People would be confused by my swearing, smoking, rebel girl attitude, clearly off the wagon every weekend, and my organic, earth-loving hippy mamma, Reiki healer, white witch, who also wanted to drive a Range Rover and live in Glastonbury.

To me, it made perfect sense. *Why can't I have success and still have strong values?* But I was also being pulled in so many directions and up against my self-made glass ceiling. The more I pushed for the material success symbols, the more it seemed to run from me. Yet, the more pain I felt from that, the more I awakened spiritually to powers inside me and to the truth that none of it mattered, it was just my ego trying to feel safe in the world.

I was however, frustrated that my funeral business was well-known, but I wasn't making enough to keep it going. As I did more Reiki and grew my intuition, it became clear that healing was my path. I was becoming magically wiser by the second, but I couldn't let go of the business.

"Try to separate your need to validate your own success through your business. Your business is a business," Yoda suggested.

But I couldn't see what he was saying. I was blind to my own issues and didn't want to explore what was going on inside.

*****

Going deep into the shadows

To go to our full potential, we have to unlearn everything we knew to be true about ourselves and our world. We have to be prepared to visit the dark places of our soul, unravel the pain of the past that is numbed by distractions and addictions. We need to freefall into the abyss. We have to learn to see who we are beyond the many masks we have created and face the fears we have been running from so we can find peace.

Teachers will come in many ways. Sometimes strangers who walk in and out of your life in a heartbeat, leaving you wisdom to chew on. They come as fleeting conversations. They are people who show us new ways of thinking and being. Some teachers are those who awaken pain and struggle in our lives. They can hurt us, shame us, and in doing so, bring gifts of awareness. Some take us down dark paths, show us the shadows of our soul, and illuminate the truth of who we are as a whole.

It is only when we are older, wiser, and stood at the top of the mountain of our life that we can see why all that happened had to happen. It is from the summit that we look back and can see the dots, joining up, creating the pathway to our destiny, our fate, one we choose of our own free will. This is wisdom. Once we have learned a wisdom, it becomes an energy we carry for the rest of our lives, and part of our service to the world. We become the teachers for others, the messengers. In stepping back and joining all the dots together, we see how we each help others grow, pushing towards a bigger picture, a soul purpose. To push us in the direction of our soul purpose, we need to awaken the lesson our soul needs to move along our path.

Along the way, there are many callings. Along the way, you are called every day. There will be deceptions before the bigger picture, and even when the bigger picture comes into view, it won't be what you think.

***

CHAPTER 8

RUPTURE AND REIKI

Shocked to death

YODA'S WORDS ECHOED in my mind, "You need to stop, Lou. You're creating chaos on top of chaos. Stop everything before the Universe stops you."

But I carried on putting more coal into the engine of that runaway train throughout the summer of 2012. On the outside, it looked amazing. *Look how fast I can go, look how fast I can go, yes to fixing your problems, yes to meetings, yes to more jobs, yes to covering every radio show, yes to seeking my success, yes to looking after everyone's kids, yes to going to every party, yes to one more rum and Coke, yes to one more cigarette, yes to abusing my body and staying up all night.*

Sometimes I would find a moment of stillness and visit Harry at the office. We would sit smoking under the magnolia tree outside our tiny office and watch the world go by, laughing about how the other half lived with their Bentleys and Range Rovers. This affluent Tudor market town, the home of our business, the façade of all things successful, was a town where everyone aspired to be more than they were and never let their guard down. Fast cars, flash bars, high-end shops, high-end companies, fake plastic people, and a snobbery around it that we bought into; it was hard not to feel inferior and want to be a part of it.

We were out of cigarettes.

"I'll get some now. I've gotta go get Bella from Nat's and then do the school run."

"I'll come with you," Harry said, "I want to grab a bottle of Coke."

"Ugh, I can't actually believe you still drink that stuff. They're an evil company."

"Do you have to have an opinion on everything I eat and drink? You drink it every weekend with your rum anyway," Harry teased.

"Yeah, well, it doesn't count if it's mixed with booze!" I laughed. "Ahhh, what a beautiful day," I said, feeling the vibes. "Stay here while I finish my cigarette, then I'll go in."

"No, it's okay. I'll go. Won't be a sec."

Off he went, into the nearby shop, and as I watched him go in, out came a woman with long dark hair. She was in her forties and didn't look like she was from around here. She began screaming and shouting at a guy. *What's going on there?* I wondered. *Is she okay? Is he hurting her? Do I need to get involved?*

"What are you looking at, you whore?" she screamed at me, too close for comfort.

"No, nothing. This is nothing to do with me..." I stammered as I stepped backwards away from the situation.

"Why are you looking at him, you whore?"

She was in my face. *Where the hell is this coming from?* I stepped backwards again into the wall and she leapt forwards — her face red and angry, her hair everywhere — and grabbed me by my ponytail! I couldn't see anything, but my hands flew up to protect my neck, as she began hitting the back of my head repeatedly with her phone. It wasn't hurting me, but I couldn't move and had no idea what was happening.

I felt Harry pulling her off me. He'd seen her though the window and had run out of the shop. The guy she was with tried to restrain her and apologise, "I'm so sorry. You'd better call the police."

Harry bundled me into the shop.

"What the fuck happened? What the fuck?" he was saying as he ordered the woman behind the counter to call the police.

They were already on their way.

It was like the whole town was in the shop and I wanted to get away from everyone looking at me. I walked to the back of the room, trying to hide myself. I could hear their judgments, their dramas, their energy, their disgust. I needed to get out of here.

"I'm not being a part of this drama, Harry. Let's go."

I looked out the window to see where the woman had gone. There she was, sat on the pavement, her head in her hands. My heart hurt for her. *What has happened in her life to attack a total stranger?* I wanted to go and help her. I wanted to throw my arms around her and take away the pain inside her.

"I just want to go and give her a hug," I said.

"Don't be so fucking stupid, Lou."

I had known he would say that. I didn't argue.

"Let's go. I need to go get the kids."

Harry held the door and there was the guy that the woman had been with earlier, looking at a loss for what to do.

"Are you okay?" I asked. My heart felt for him too.

"Yeah, are you? I'm so sorry. I just need to get her home to her mum," he said shaking.

That seemed a weird thing to say. She was older than me.

"I'm sorry for what's happened. I hope you get the help she needs," I said.

I wished he didn't feel so bad. I could see he was a good guy. I put my head down, trying to shrink as small as I could as we walked passed her.

"Why the fuck are you talking to him, you whore?" she screamed as we passed, "Oi, you fucking whore."

She must have got up, because she was behind us. I could feel her. Harry turned around to meet her raging face and she spat at him. I had never felt his gentle giant body tense with pure anger before, and as I felt the muscle on his forearm tighten, I gripped him tight and pulled him closer.

"Let's go, let's go," I said quietly.

I pulled him forward, and, glued to each other, we tried walking away as fast as we could. Within seconds, the woman yanked my hair from behind, spun me and hit me. I slammed to the ground with her on top of me.

Commotion, blank, surrender. I can't feel anything. I'm no longer in this world. Someone is going to save me from wherever I am right now.

And then I heard it. God's voice, deep, protective, divine. *You have everything you need right here.*

I felt Harry's arms on my body, pulling me back into the world. I looked up and saw him. Then three other guys, holding her back. She was screaming, furious, her face distorted with rage. She wanted me dead. I could feel she wanted to kill me. I had to get away from her. Being anywhere near her was fuelling her fire. The world was slow, people all around me, but I needed to get away. There was a doorway into a pub. I grabbed Harry's hand and fled for survival.

Standing in the middle of the pub, I was a trapped animal trying to find its way out. I saw the door out the other side, and with everyone looking, ran away. I sat down in the office sobbing, then went for a smoke outside. That's when I realised I couldn't breathe properly. As the adrenalin started to wear off, I noticed I was injured. The pain down the right side of my body got progressively worse.

The police turned up. Then the paramedic told me I'd fractured my ribs.

"Nothing you can do about it except go home and rest up."

I was overcome with exhaustion, and then guilt for feeling so weak. It wasn't like I was stabbed or anything. I didn't understand why I was so tired. Once home, I got into bed and fell asleep, supported on all sides with pillows. At midnight I woke up, unable to breathe. My ribs hurt so much that I couldn't pull myself up to get out of bed. I panicked.

"HARRY, HARRY, HARRY! Get me up, get me up! FUCK! Get me up!"

He woke and helped me up. I was unbearably hot and sweating so much I could feel the drops rolling down my back. I stripped off through the pain and stumbled towards the bathroom. I needed to cool down, so I lay on the cold tile floor. I began to shake uncontrollably, like I was having a weird out-of-body experience or seizure. Harry got down on the floor next to me and I could do nothing except stare at him, locking eyes. At that moment, he felt like my only connection to earth. The safety net he had always been in my life held in place with only our eyes. I was terrified. I thought I was dying.

"Lou, I'm going to call an ambulance."

I managed to mumble a yes, but after a few minutes, Harry saw me come round.

"I don't want an ambulance," I said, "I just want to go back to sleep."

Shock can cause death. Indeed, something died that night for me. Something that needed to die. They say, when the disciple is ready, the master will appear. That's how it felt.

I wanted to be alone, to watch the sky, to be in the stillness, in meditative silence. I went down and sat on the front doorstep, transfixed by the way the light moved from blue skies to dusk to darkness. In the background, music shuffled on random through my playlists, songs for my soul. Track after track, the Universe spoke to me, soothing the pain in my body, soothing me into new dimensions, new places inside, new worlds. I was so aware, aware of every tiny detail, in this ethereal state of bliss. The green of the grass became greener. I watched the intensity of the colours, the same as those awakened by ecstasy or 2CB, but here it was purity, a connection to Mother Earth, showing me how beautiful she was. There was so much beauty everywhere I was overwhelmed. Uncontrollable sobs rose up. It was too much, all this beauty. It touched me, as though I was seeing it for the first time.

The tears turned to sorrow. The pain gripped my bruised, broken body, and the emotions baffled me. These tears felt like sadness, but with pockets of gratitude, and I loved everything so much at the same time. My sensibility to this world was beyond anything, everything was loud, and I was delicate, desperate to absorb all that was around me, in case it broke any second.

For days, I wandered around the house in this state, aimless, too pained to do anything, too sensitive to look at a screen. I took myself back to the doorstep to watch the stars at night. I lit cigarette after cigarette, unaware of the irony that I couldn't breathe yet couldn't stop smoking. I knew in my heart that this was a call to surrender to the chaos that was unfolding in my life. It was the Universe aligning for it all to come back together again. This was a gift somehow.

Messages and emails came from every direction. All these people who loved me so much, who relied on me to be their rock, now wanted to be mine. It was beautiful to have this love. It was too much. My heart hurt. My chest contracted. Then the sobbing would take me into the darkness again, my mind unable to understand why I was crying at all. *What's wrong with me? Is this depression? The extreme highs, the lowest lows?*

The summer days were hot, but the nights had a strange mystical haze as the mists came in. I was in my usual place on the doorstep watching the world go by. The rain began to fall, dancing on my face. I raised my arms in the air joyful at this connection. Nature was holding me. I cried and laughed and danced in the garden without a care in the world.

As soon as a thought of Sandy flashed into my mind, sobs came from nowhere. I began to see the pain my best friend had been through when she'd been stabbed. We had a deep connection. I had thought I'd understood her pain at the time of her stabbing, but now I realised I'd had no idea.

How could I have? *No one truly understands unless they have been through it.* I felt sad for her suffering and guilty that I had not fully understood until now how deep her wounds went.

Propped up on pillows, I fell into a Reiki sleep. After many nights of not understanding my tears and emotions, I began to find some peace, knowing my guardian angels were with me helping my body. I woke the next morning with a desperate need to see Sandy. I had never had a moment in my life where I had needed anyone other than Harry in that way, but I needed her more than anyone right now. She came right away. I curled into her arms like a baby. We sobbed together.

"I'm so sorry, Sandy. I had no idea what you were feeling when you were stabbed. I still don't. And it overwhelmed me that I could only understand a little bit of the pain you went through. I thought I was there for you, but I realised you were still alone in your emotional state. How could I have ever truly understood? I feel awful, because this is nothing like what happened to you, yet I'm either a wreck or in bliss."

Sandy's voice lowered.

"You know we're so connected. Our energies are entwined some way. I spoke to a medium the other day and she said the same. She thinks we're healing each other's stories on some soul level though our own life lessons. You helped me so much, babe. You shouldn't be so hard on yourself. I'm doing okay. Everything for a reason..."

In that moment, I sensed something, and she knew I sensed it too. An awkwardness came in.

"Lou, I need to tell you something."

My heart twisted. I read her thoughts before she could speak.

"Don't say it, Sand. I know what you're going to say."

"I didn't want to tell you today, but I can't hide anything from you. It's just strange that it's happened now after a year of waiting. Our visas for Australia have just arrived. We are moving in a few weeks."

Though my spirit sank at the idea of losing my best friend of over 15 years, equally I knew this was right for her and wanted her to be happy. The stabbing had been like a curveball in her life, turning her direction towards Australia. In many ways, the attack I'd experienced was serving as a curveball in my own life.

"Yoda warned me. He told me the Universe would stop me if I didn't stop myself. Then this. Maybe the divine had it lined up for us all along!" I smiled. "You deserve a new life, Sandy. Go to Australia with your darling husband and make the babies you would not have made if you'd stayed in London. I'll be fine."

I knew there was a path opening up to me too.

***

Into the earth

As soon as she left, I felt flat. The realisation she was leaving felt like change was coming at me from every direction, even in subtle currents. I was lost in the void inside the house, so I felt pulled to go meditate in the back garden. *Oh this fucking garden*, I thought, looking at the chaos that always overwhelmed me. It needed thousands spent on it. I rarely sat it in, even though it was tranquil and the wildness of it was somewhat comforting.

I was guided to sit on the broken step in the sun. My meditation position was far from ideal, knees too high, ribs aching, but it took no time to transport myself to a place of stillness. It was so quick it was like I was being taken there.

I envisioned myself in a jungle, walking down a path at the end of which was a cave. I approached and entered the cave through a huge wooden door. In the centre of the darkness was Archangel Gabriel and my Reiki guide Gupta. They took an arm each and walked me towards the back wall. I felt a sudden force of fear. Gabriel and Gupta held me tight and I couldn't move. I was confused by their energy; normally so gentle, now they were almost forceful, like I had no choice but to go with them. I didn't even have time to resist as I was pushed through a hole in the wall into a dark tunnel.

Next, I was standing in a smaller cave, dark with an enormous blue crystal in the centre on a raised sacred stone. When I looked to my left, there was an imposing shadow of a male figure in a cloak with a hood. The right side of his face was revealed to me and I could barely believe it was Jesus. Suddenly, I became overwhelmed with peace, love and a sense of something greater, a sense of coming home, having been lost. He opened his arms and I fell into them. He held me close to his chest until I was ready to look at him. When I did, he spoke.

"Lou, you must learn to be comfortable with people looking up to you and wanting to love you. Welcome the worship. By shaking it off and thinking you're not worthy, it hurts those trying to love you."

I knew what he meant. Many people had been putting me on a pedestal in regards to my healing and intuition, and simply for being me. I would brush it off. I couldn't take compliments so I would downplay my talents, even act a bit stupid, leaving me and the other person feeling awkward.

"Imagine if I had rejected your embrace saying I wasn't worthy of that love. How would you have felt?"

I realised then what he was teaching me. He showed me how it felt to receive love when people looked up to me for guidance and leadership. I had to learn how to be this for others, to be comfortable in my power.

He took my hand and we knelt in front of the crystal. I made an oath, promising to bring peace and healing to everyone I met, to live life with contentment, to inspire others, and to remain open to receiving. Jesus embraced me again and kissed my forehead.

"Remember, when you let others love you as you love them, it feels good for them too."

Then I was on a wooden bench outside the cave, Archangel Gabriel holding my left hand and Gupta my right. We sat in stillness together, letting the lesson flow through me, waiting for acceptance of what and who I needed to be.

The wind blew around my body. I could feel the end of the vision coming, pushing away. I came around to the garden and the first thing I noticed was my pain had gone. I was surprised only 20 minutes had passed, because it had felt like a lifetime. I wanted to tell everyone about it, but how could I admit this? *I mean, Jesus?! I'm not even Christian.*

That evening I tried to explain the lesson to Harry. He humoured me, but I could see he was not interested in anything to do with Christianity. I wanted him to *get* the magnitude of what I had just experienced. It felt so radical, although I knew the lesson was going to take time to flow through me. For a start, my ego was screaming, *Who the fuck do you think you are?* Still, the message sat within me.

Who am I to put myself down? To shr
for whom?

***

Yoda called, like he was in tune with me. He always knew what was going on and what I needed, in the same way I knew what others needed. It was beautiful to have someone looking out for me spiritually.

"Lou, you're going inwards and this is a rich time for you. Journal every day. Listen to yourself and see yourself. There will be many insights to uncover, and as you do, you will begin to rise again."

I had mantras keeping me here, present in the moment. Every time my mind wanted to beat myself up for not being enough, not doing enough and generally creating drama in my head, I regained control of my mind. It was time to fine-tune my attitude. At least in part, I felt I had released myself from a cage, a cage of my own making, where my mind was trapped in obsessive thinking. But there was still so much more work to do.

The angels were around me all the time now. I felt them on my skin. My whole body tingled. I started speaking to them directly, just talking to them, wishing I knew what they were saying all the time. I knew they were guiding me through my darkness. I knew I was being called.

Two months after the attack, I was still a bit out of it, though on the surface I looked fine. Yoda started teaching me to mentor myself, question myself, so I could learn to get to the truth of my own issues. *How do I feel? Why do I want to do this work? What are my true intentions? Who do I want to be? How can I change my patterns?* I wasn't there yet. It was hard learning to ask myself deeper questions all the time, both in my mind and in my journal, but it was beginning to help me unravel what was going on in my head.

One of the main teachings I took from Yoda at that time was respecting Harry's space, not forcing him down my spiritual path. Sometimes I just wished he would do his own 'personal work' and then he could come with me. I wanted him to feel what I felt. But that expectation caused tension between us.

Despite the ongoing work, I could see I had changed. Finances were still not great, but we were dealing with them better. I felt calmer in myself and something weird was going on with Harry. He was changing too. It started simply — with not putting sugar in his coffee! I'd been bugging him about it for years, but I'd stopped lately, and then he made the choice himself. It felt like the start of something. Harry had been more helpful than usual around the house. We were keeping on top of things and I didn't have to ask. He seemed happy and relaxed. I thought perhaps he was starting to see his own power, so was acting more powerfully. He was the master of his own universe. And I was too.

Harry had gone back to teasing and being playful with me. It had been months since he'd been like that — picking me up and snogging my face off. He was less stressed with work these days. Something about him was more confident, less worried what people thought. He had been way more on the ball with clients too, putting in stronger boundaries, not just saying yes all the time. He had started to listen to me. Not roll his eyes!

Yoda was right. Harry was on his own journey. All I had to do was 'be the change' and follow my own path. I could do that, surely.

***

Accepting our own different journeys

I wanted to do my Reiki Masters course. The signs were everywhere. It was going to cost £500 and I would be away for three nights. The usual blockage of money was coming up. *I know Harry isn't going to want me to go and he will use money as an excuse, so I'll need to navigate this conversation!*

A boozy dinner with Harry turned into a full-on argument. Tensions rose between us.

"You're not supporting me in something I know I need to do, Harry," I shouted.

Harry blew his top. It was so rare to see him do that, I had to hide my laughter. It was normally me acting like this.

I walked away from the dinner table and went upstairs, where I sat on the end of our bed staring at the old lava lamp, while Harry sat downstairs watching TV. All I wanted to do was go down and curl up in his arms on the sofa, but I forced myself not to move. I was *always* the one who went to make up and say sorry. As I got up to go into the bathroom, he came upstairs, grabbed me and kissed me hard. He kissed me in a way that could only come from passionate desperation. Without saying anything, we were hugging tight. Few words were said between us. Nothing really could be said. Neither of us understood what we were arguing about.

bed and lay looking in each other's eyes. He
as going to cry, but I saw he was just bone-
sad in there and I didn't think he even knew
why. I knew why. *All the talk of Reiki Masters is triggering
him*, I thought. *He doesn't like me changing and doing the
Reiki Masters is going to change me. It's going to take me
somewhere he can't go.*

We had the most beautiful sex, releasing us emotionally,
and passed out asleep. A few hours later, I stirred and
reached for his hand. Within seconds, he'd pulled me on top
of him, and in a half-dream state, we were making deep love
again.

I had been so self-absorbed in my own spirituality and
healing that I'd forgotten to ask what was important to him,
to see his needs, to know how work was, to understand his
sense of purpose. I resolved to make more effort to be
interested. I passed on some new knowledge from Yoda to
help Harry's business, and he was inspired by it, empowered
even. He seemed to be accepting I would have to go away to
do my Reiki Masters. And yet, we weren't really talking
about it.

I acknowledged that my choice to go deeper into
spirituality was changing things between us. I realised it was
going to stir up some stuff. Some days were not perfect
between us, but rather than getting upset about it, I simply
allowed those days to be what they needed to be, reminding
myself that everything was temporary.

"You know, babe, it's time I closed the funeral company
down. Technology has caught up. People can do this stuff on
their phones now. And I know I'm meant to be a healer and
coach. With my Reiki Masters, it would mean being able to
do much more transformational healing."

"And what about real credentials, Lou? What are you going to say when people ask you for those?"

I took a long, deep breath and centred myself. I looked at him in the eyes, gathering all my power back to me, and held the energy of stillness, presence and compassion.

"I've realised my energy alone is enough, Harry."

I spoke in a grounded way, beyond my usual childlike excitement. I showed him who I could be when I was fully centred, conscious and in my power.

"My example is my credentials."

I let him feel my presence. I held the silence and waited. I watched him light up as he got it. I saw his pride. He knew what I'd learnt. And I was proud of myself. Finally, I believed in myself and I knew he saw it too.

"Harry, I'll work for you three days a week if you pay for my mentoring."

Amazed that he'd agreed, we connected in a new way.

***

I saw a heron on the way home from Sunday lunch with our friends. It flew right in front of us on the motorway. It was the third one in a week. I'd never seen one before and now they were everywhere. I found out that herons represent the acceptance of Mother Nature's flow and rhythms. They are normally seen as a good omen, unless you read the Christian texts. Not so flowing and peaceful there; more a struggle with the devil!

That would be about right actually, because I'd had the devil in me all week, wanting to just eat, party hard and get into mischief with Harry. Otherwise, we'd had a great vibe going on at home. Harry, the girls and I colouring in and playing together contentedly. Harry had been absorbing my want for consciousness and my trust in myself had begun shining out. We'd talked so much lately and were so connected. He would listen and get inspired by what I was saying about teaching consciousness, mindfulness and meditation. It was just wonderful how contented and grateful we all were.

Harry and I put the girls to bed and then got back into our usual Friday night party mode. The 'fuck it' monster was around and I was off the wagon, smoking, drinking and being wild! The photos from a boudoir shoot that I had modelled for a friend had come through and Harry could not stop telling me how proud he was. All night, we chatted, laughed and played tunes. We saw the most amazing halo around the moon, and as we stood outside watching it, he told me he felt like the luckiest man in the world. I felt like the luckiest woman in the world too. *I have everything.*

Next day, we had a lazy morning in bed cuddling, while the girls played and popped in every now and then. I felt so lucky, again, to have such a laid-back, fun-loving, affectionate environment. Sometimes I had to remind myself that this is unique. Not everyone had this. I was loving the passion and intimacy Harry and I had these days and always. I enjoyed the affection, and adored the pure love the girls had from us, for us and for each other. It made us laugh hearing them play, listening to Avalon's wonderful empathy and her sense of responsibility towards Bella. *This is what matters, not what we don't have. This is priceless.*

On the way into town, another heron sailed over the road up ahead. *A heron! Again! What does it mean? It's a sign, I know it. A sign of flow and prosperity.* It glided in front of us just as I was telling myself that consciousness is the path to all this joy I'd been feeling.

And that's just the point, isn't it? Becoming aware means more flow.

***

CHAPTER 9

PURPOSE PEEKS THROUGH

The definition of success

I NEEDED A SESSION with Yoda. I was on the edge of something, but we didn't have any cash. I asked if I could pay when some money came in. He replied to my message, agreeing to do the session, but with a caveat.

"So long as you use the strategy and goal-setting tools we've talked about in the past few months to figure out how you're going to pay me back. It's not that I need the money, but if I gave it to you for free, you wouldn't see the value in it or do the work."

Money is energy. It teaches us more about ourselves than we realise. And Yoda knew this. I booked the session.

For six months, I had been up and down, knowing I had to let go of my funeral business, even though I was attached to it. I shed light on why I didn't want to let it go. I'd had so many hopes and dreams for it, and it felt like failure to close the doors. *Who will I be without a successful business?* I had done what I'd set out to do: helped so many people celebrate life and made some big changes in the industry.

Now it was time to let it go. And Yoda would help me find the last hook holding me back from moving into the future. I dialled his number.

"Lou, I'm curious. Why are you always so broke? Do you value what you do? Would you pay someone to do what you do?" Yoda quizzed me.

"If I had the money, I would."

"If you value what you do, why can't you take money from people for it?"

"It just feels weird," I said, unable to pinpoint it.

"Who loses out when you don't take money for your work?" he asked.

"I do," I said.

"Who else?" He went silent for a while, then repeated his question, "Who else loses out when you don't take money for what you deliver — something you value, and do with all your time, effort and love?"

My eyes dropped. I felt ashamed. I realised what he was saying. Harry and the kids lost out.

"The client wins in this deal, so you operate a you-lose-they-win mindset. Is that balanced? No! So, what would be a win-win?" Yoda pressed.

"I do a good job and they pay for the value of that work," I admitted.

Yoda smiled.

"I'm wondering what memories you have around money."

I laughed and told him a funny story about when my dad picked me up one Saturday morning. Mum had said I should ask him to help towards fixing my computer. It was going to cost £70. I'd never asked Dad for anything at that time. He had never paid us a penny. Mum had to prep me, telling me to say, "Mum said can you contribute towards the computer." So I got in the car and that's what I did, but my dad just screamed at me. It was so random. He yelled that I was selfish. He said all I ever did was take, take, take; that all he ever did was give to me; that I needed to learn to give back rather than always be taking. (It was fucking ridiculous, because I *had* never and *could* never ask anyone for anything. I felt so guilty that I cost people money every month simply by being alive.) My dad was driving like a maniac, when I realised we weren't going the normal way. The next thing I knew he was dropping me back off at Mum's saying, "Get out! I never want to see you again!"

When Mum asked what on earth I was doing there, I'd fallen to the ground, but sort of watched myself do it. I'd thought, *Stop being such a drama queen and get up, Lou.* Everything felt weird because my mum got onto the floor and pulled me into her arms. I didn't feel like I needed this sympathy, feeling ashamed at my overreaction. It wasn't such a big deal — was it?

Yoda was quiet. I just laughed.

Softly, Yoda spoke, "That's a sad story, Lou. I feel sad listening to that story."

"Nawww, it was nothing. I was fine," I said brushing it off.

"Lou, this story has not been completed. You have not fully felt this. It's okay to feel this."

Silent tears rolled down my face. I was fighting it.

"It's no big deal. God, people have so much worse than me."

"This isn't about anyone else. This is about you, your story," Yoda said. "You have permission to feel it now."

"By feeling the unfelt pains of our past, we heal the patterns that hold us stuck. We become open to new possibilities. This is a core belief from your past telling you that you do not deserve money, that you're a burden to your parents and you are not worthy of asking for or receiving money. There will be many more beliefs in there holding you back, but for now, you must honour that child who was hurt by her father."

I ended the call, and went to bed and cried. I was distant from Harry, and when he put up his walls too, that made me cry even more. Yoda texted and suggested processing it by journaling every day that week to shift my money blocks. At 22:22 on the Friday night, I got an email:

I know you do funerals, but it's my husband's 40th next month and we would like to use your services. Budget not an issue, just time. Needs to be ready in six weeks. Can you help?

I had never had an email like that before, so direct and willing! Wow, I had manifested a client who valued all that I did... This would be the biggest project I'd ever done. I took it. I hired staff. And at the end of the truly amazing event six weeks later, I walked away with huge profits and an incredibly happy client. Most of all, I felt successful!

Deep in conversation with one of my best friends a week later, we were discussing where our focus was and what we wanted in life. For the first time ever, I could honestly say clearly what that was. And it wasn't 10 successful businesses, a fleet of cars, and an obnoxious mansion with 12 pools and a yacht!

It was much simpler than that...

To live a life of purpose, contentment and happiness so that I inspire others.

***

The money went as quickly as it came. When you have deep money issues stemming from childhood, it takes time to heal it. Especially if your issues are wrapped around a belief system that you don't deserve money — as mine were — it's near impossible to keep hold of it. It will go as quickly as it came and life will remain the same.

I had a deep belief that I couldn't 'have it all.' Somewhere in my belief system, I had a story running: if I had money, I couldn't have love too. That it had to be one or the other. Some people have it the other way around and sabotage their relationships because they don't feel they deserve love if they have success. We're all fighting an inner battle of some kind.

I had a belief system that went something like: I was a burden; if I had money, I must give it away. I also had a childhood of feeling deeply responsible for my father 'not paying a penny towards me.' I felt so guilty because he had no money either. Sometimes he would offer me pocket money and I just couldn't take it. I would try to give it back to him because the guilt of taking it was too painful. He used to laugh at me and say, "Just take it, Lou. Go buy some sweets!" He was totally unaware of the storm going on inside me. To calm that storm, I would go and buy sweets for me and all the neighbours, so that I didn't have money anymore and would feel better.

Learning to hold on to money was going to take some deeper healing, so I forgave myself for having spent the money on overdrafts and a family ski holiday, and for manifesting loads of extra bills that swallowed up the bit I wanted to save. *It is what it is,* I kept reminding myself when the shame and guilt kicked in. *The Universe is abundant and it will come around again.*

We were away skiing on our first ever family holiday when it happened. As we hung out with doctors, lawyers — you know, real adults — the conversation over the dinner table turned to our work.

"What is it that you do, Lou?"

"I'm a radio presenter and a healer," I said with pride. There was nothing in me that wanted to talk about the business... a sign I was beginning to let it go.

One by one, our newfound friends asked questions. I could feel their enchantment with what I was saying and Harry's enchantment with the way these people were looking at his wife. This was what I needed: him to see 'normal folk' validating and respecting me and my wisdom. And here it was. When I spoke, people wanted to hear what I had to say. Wherever I went, people wanted to be around me. Not just that. Many opened up their darkest secrets and deepest wounds, and what came out of my mouth seemed to bring solace and healing.

The holiday brought a new sense of freedom. The girls were in kids' clubs, and for us, the booze was flowing. Harry and I were like a comedy duo all week, outwitting each other, joking around, playing together, and ending every night belly laughing at the bar.

But the frequent intoxication was numbing my now-sensitive senses. And one particular day, the hangover was horrid. I had never in my life had a hangover so bad that I was unable to ski. I wanted to stop all the booze but I knew Harry loved that part of me. Everyone loved Party Lou!

That night, I placed my hands on my body and fell into a Reiki journey deep into the mountains. At last, a message from my angels came through: *You will become more than you ever knew possible by the time you are 40.*

In the vision, the angels showed me how people gravitated towards me; my light like a sweetness in their life. I would be somewhere I never dreamed in just seven years. I would go into politics when I was older. I laughed inwardly, *Yeah right!* Yet I knew I needed to let go of my self-chastising around academic capabilities. I could see now that didn't define me. On this holiday, I'd been mixing with professionals and businessmen, all of whom I could relate to and had the ability to speak to on many levels. *I have as much value as they do.*

The next day, Harry and I sat on a chairlift with quiet all around us. It was changeover day in the resort and the only four people we could see were on the seat in front. Far in the distance in a mountain ravine, we saw something flying. Simultaneously, we gasped.

"What's that over there?" I asked Harry.

Whatever it was, it was huge.

"Must be someone in one of those flying suits, like in that Red Bull Extreme Sports video last night."

"I don't fucking think so, babe," I laughed, "They don't float on the thermals. Look!"

"Jesus!" exclaimed Harry, "It's an eagle!"

And it was. Soaring above us in the sky was a magnificent golden eagle. My heart called her closer, *Come, come, come closer.* The bird presented herself to us. I had been holding my breath, I realised, and tears were flowing down my cheeks. I could not explain the emotion she was raising in me other than a deep connection and knowing — an inner knowing of something huge, but an inability to see it fully. The details on the underneath of the eagle's belly and feathers were outstanding. It felt like a dream and I knew I had called her to me. She was the most incredible natural being I had seen in my life. Then just like that, she flew away.

Harry and I remained in silent wonder. *Wow! Did that even happen?*

I knew she was my spirit guide, showing me to keep flying high, to see the whole world with wisdom and grace.

***

Seeking life purpose

I left for my Reiki Masters weekend. I could still feel a little resistance from Harry, though he didn't say anything. He just didn't jump for joy.

"I need to do this, Harry. I need to go away and learn this, not just for my work, but for our girls. I can teach them this power. I can teach you too," I said as I raised my arms around his neck and kissed him. "Please stop being so grumpy about it. It's one weekend. And I'll come back super-powered!"

The weekend was still and quiet. I knew this was the perfect start to 2013. My Reiki Master was sweet and gentle, gifting me a deeper connection to the Reiki so I could pass it on to my kids. But I was still waiting for clear guidance from the angels on what to do next for my soul purpose, as if it was going to appear on ancient scrolls with step-by-step instructions! I still hadn't learned that life and awakening wasn't like that. Life unfolds in each moment. Sometimes we just need to let go of having to know and let the flow guide us.

My attunements were gentle, but I saw the unlocking of a complex door. The calm of the weekend was what I needed most, space to be on my own, which I never had at home. Stillness brought me back to earth. I saw how I'd been operating: with my higher self during the week, then with my lower self at weekends, getting smashed with Harry and abusing my body with booze. The guides were telling me not to be shy about my true abilities anymore; to share my gift, but also accept that people are different; to stop trying to get them to follow *my* path.

The journey home was beautiful. I could feel the sun on my face as it was setting. I was fully connected to the world, immersed in feelings of hope and joy. I came home to Harry and we made love. After, I did Reiki on him and saw us walking in the heart of a beautiful woodland, on the same path. There were angels around us and a white horse. I had an inner knowing about what this meant. I had to come back to him wholly, to learn how to teach without preaching. *I am a teacher now but my journey has only just begun,* I thought.

I passed on the gift of Reiki to them. I attuned him. I attuned the girls. He could feel it. They could feel it rushing out of their hands like beams of light. This was a new level for me. A new level for us all, like playing with a new toy.

With Harry, we would lie in bed together our arms looped in an infinity sign over our heads sending Reiki around. He would put his hands on me and send it to my back. He was good. Really good. Although he didn't like to make a big deal of it. He was still a man of science after all.

Avalon would talk of seeing angels.

"It's like light floats around my body and wraps me up in cuddles."

Despite this new level, I was still waiting for *something* to happen. I just didn't know what. I knew I was here for something important. I knew it was all coming. I had beautiful visions and knew there was a message waiting, just over the horizon, but nothing came. Nada. Not for days, weeks, months. Yet I was waiting.

While I waited for *something* to happen, we had a particularly crazy period, our calendar filled with parties. With it came copious drinking... resulting in days on end in bed feeling broken. I wanted to stop, but everyone loved Party Lou... even I loved Party Lou. Yet my body was screaming out. I felt so guilty for the amount I drank at weekends but couldn't see a way out. I'd resigned myself to the idea that it was never going to change. It was just the culture of our friends and family.

One day, a clear message vibrated through me. *Call your Reiki Master and ask for distance healing.* Despite the fact I didn't have the money for a session, despite the fact I could heal myself, I did it.

"I feel so lost waiting for something to happen," I told him. "It's like my purpose is waiting for me, but I fear I'm not good enough to do whatever I am meant to do here on earth."

The session started with one hand on my heart and the other on my stomach. I channelled Reiki to myself, but soon realised I was here to receive, so took my hands off and placed them by my sides. Surrendering to what would be, I let David do his work.

My Reiki playlist played in my ears and I knew he had started. The warmth of the energy washed over my body. Deep down, I anticipated something big, but I had no idea it would be *this* big. Images flashed before me so fast that it was hard to catch what I was seeing, like a movie of split-second clips.

I was a young girl, skipping... There was Gupta, my Reiki guide, holding my hand... The top of a mountain... Dragons eating dead things... Everywhere, I saw energy...

Then I was at a beach, kneeling at the sea, washing my hair... The sea, a liquid golden light... A sister in a headscarf, a nurse but a nun too... Was it me?

Then I was old. I sat in a chair. I had to face myself, but I didn't want to see. I looked very, very old and very, very lonely. Was that me? It was me.

From seeing myself, I knew I would have to learn more, to experience loss and loneliness, a small price to pay when I hadn't experienced it in my younger years. I would have to experience that feeling sometime, my darkest fear. That was the message. I prayed I could embrace the feeling of loss, if it came.

At that point, the vision went crazy. I began to transition into another world, like I was flying through blackness at high speed, yet in the blackness there were triangles of light. I flew through the lights, through space, through lines upon lines of red and green. Here I was, but it was not me. It was my consciousness transporting me, passing through the Universe at light speed to other dimensions.

Boom!

There I was in an old room, almost like a church. I was at the front of an audience being crowned by kings.

I recall my ego observing this vision and chipping in a thought, *Who the fuck do you think you are being crowned?* It was a distant thought and I gave it no room to creep in.

Instead, I felt the worship. I was Guinevere. My ego again, *Who the fuck is Guinevere? Isn't that King Arthur's wife?* But then came the moment I was crowned and another voice inside me — a strong fatherly voice — was more prominent.

"You are chosen," it said.

I could see the crowns of the kings who were watching and angels all around us. Then the crown on my head with a white sparkly stone almost the size of the vision itself. On my finger was a tiny ruby ring. I could see my heaven, as I'd imagined it as a child, with a room full of screens, where I could watch my life back in little moments, soundtracked by all my favourite music.

The vision changed again and I was atop a pyramid, my body split in half, my blood pouring out and being cleansed as it passed through a tunnel of light. The golden light poured into me, replacing my blood, and dragons flew above.

I was beginning to come back and had a sensation of understanding of the lessons of these past few months. They were about learning to receive.

And looking after myself.

***

"This is big," I told Harry.

Something had happened! He listened intently, taking me seriously. Maybe he listened because he understood the Reiki now, or maybe my energy was more commanding since the vision. As I shared with him, I felt a weight lift from my soul, relief that I had a purpose and it was coming. I didn't understand it at all, but I knew something was happening at last.

"Babe, I need you to hold me close but also let me go. I have wings. I need to fly now. You are my twin flame. I have pure love for you — the purest love there is. We are like two angels. We fly together in unique companionship. We fly and learn and grow. We get lost in our dreams and make mistakes together, knowing that the safety net of each other is always there. We are connected in ways that many only dream of, love and attraction always strong and beautiful and pure. Together we are uncomplicated and true, trusting and forgiving. The balance is unbelievable and magical, spiritual and real. We live, we love, we feel pain, we feel joy. And with every feeling, we learn and we grow."

He watched me, the way he did when he didn't understand but he didn't care, because I could say anything and he would love me. No matter what. To death and beyond.

***

CHAPTER 10

WAKE UP, WORLD

Kicking addictions

YOU WAKE UP AND see how you've been behaving... Unconscious. Unaware. Driven by your addictions. Shopping, TV, sex, food, alcohol, nicotine, drugs, social media, desire, porn, toxic relationships, moaning, game play, drama. Whatever your vice, there will be one that is yours. When you see it and your drive to change is bigger than your drive to addiction, you become aware that this vice has control over you.

And then you see what else has control over you. Your own opinions are not really yours; they have come from your parents, from religions, from the media telling you what to think, telling you what the world is like. You wake up to the fact that none of it is true at all. Fear of failure, fear of rejection, fear of the world ending, it's all just distracting you from the beauty around you. You begin to see that we have, for a long time, been divided and separated, been conditioned to strive not for love and connection, but for material wealth that never fulfils the emptiness inside, no matter how rich we become. You see that we raise kids to have strong grades but weak minds. They are empty shells, disconnected from the earth, locked into screens.

You start to question why. *Why? Why am I doing this? What does it bring me? Why do I need it?* You start to wake up. You start to realise you have no control over yourself, because your mind has control over you and your mind is controlled by others. Once you know that, though, you start to take back control of yourself, of your mind. You go deeper into your soul.

Your awakening begins...

You have less fear. You smile more. You trust that there is something greater, something that vibrates with the energy of love. With every smile, you begin to connect. With every action you take, you know in your heart of hearts that this is good for you and done with integrity. Every thought is pure and positive. There are no lies or fears of what people think.

You feel lighter now. So free you could fly. You speak lighter too. You are alive and connected.

You may shake your head because it all feels too good to be true. Then everything starts to come your way. Things fall into place. That's when you know. You're in the flow.

Then the next level comes... Responsibility. Because what was once trapping you is still trapping our earth and all its children. Your soul purpose awakens. *What am I here for?* Deep down, you know you are here for a greater purpose. To be in service.

***

Closure and compassion

It was a year to the day after the attack, when we were called into court. It wasn't my choice to prosecute the woman who had attacked me, who I now knew was called Kath. The state was prosecuting and we had to stand witness. I was nervous. I didn't even have any clothes to wear to court. My wardrobe consisted of three pairs of denim hot pants and three different tops. I didn't really own anything suitable, so I found an old, floaty, summer dress and felt totally out of place when we arrived at the courts at 8am.

Kath walked through the doors and sat in the waiting room. We were the only people there. I would never have recognised her, but Harry pointed her out and my heart began to race. Fear, sadness, I felt all the feelings I had forgotten I had felt a year before.

I headed off to the loo and noticed I couldn't quite catch my breath. l sat there sobbing when I heard the door go. I knew it was her. I took a deep breath and walked outside. She was by the basins.

"Hey, are you Kath?" She looked right though me, surprised by my question. She didn't know who I was.

"Erm yes, why?"

I just looked at her and said, "I'm Louise."

Her face dropped.

"It's okay. It's okay," I said. "Look, there is something I wanted to do that day, but I couldn't. Can I just give you a hug?"

She looked at me with tears in her eyes and we hugged. She told me how she was going to lose her daughter if they prosecuted, that she was bipolar and that her meds had been all messed up. We talked and I knew the woman I was with was not the woman who had attacked me that day. I wished her well.

Harry didn't want to stay for the whole of the case. He was adamant, worried and cross with me for having spoken to Kath in the toilet, more out of fear for me being easily manipulated and sucked into sob stories than anything else.

"Just say your statement and then we can leave, stay out of the drama."

"No, I want to stay for the whole thing. If you don't, you can go and I'll get a cab back."

He knew he couldn't push me.

The judge began by sharing his surprise, "Well I never, exactly a year to the day."

I was not surprised. Synergies like this were my norm now. I watched the energy of the judge move and shift. I watched Kath's energy shift, from her position in the glass box. She was no longer the woman I'd met in the toilet. She looked hostile, cold. I didn't want to see her like that. I knew in my heart it was her protection.

The court went on for some time. It was a tough decision, but the facts were that she was totally unsupported by the state with her mental health and therefore she was not guilty of ABH.

I was joyful, I didn't want her sent down, but I could see her coldness. Harry wanted me to leave right away but I refused.

"No! I need to see her."

She was let out of the glass box surrounded by lawyers and legal people. They were all looking at me as if I was the baddie, but I wasn't going to move. I wanted to see her.

They had no choice but to come past me, I was standing in the door. They surrounded her, protecting her from me.

"I just want to speak with her," I mumbled as I tried to move into the group of men.

It was as if the whole world stopped. Everyone in the court room held their breath, like the calm before the storm.

I reached out my hand, and the lights went on, I saw her face soften, she could see me, beyond her mindfuck, she could see my light. I reached in and hugged her, whispering to her 'you're free now, I wish you all the blessings, may you be free of this and get all the help you need to rise up.'

She smiled and we both cried as she was pushed through the door by her lawyers.

Harry looked at me, grabbed my hand and we walked out.

He kept looking at me, "Lou! Do you know what you did in there? I don't think anyone had ever seen such a thing. The whole room was staring in awe! I'm so proud of you. You were right. We had to stay today. I'm so proud of you, I think you've changed lives and not just hers. I don't believe some of them have ever witnessed such compassion."

For me, it was normal, it wasn't such a big thing. But for Harry to see the reactions of others... it hit him hard. He hit a new level of trust and respect in me that day. We went home and I went to bed, energetically exhausted by the day, only to wake up later that evening to an epically long post on Facebook — for someone who rarely posted anything he was telling the world how proud he was of me and how today had blown his mind!

Old habits die hard. Old habits make us die hard!

We'd have shit dinners on Fridays. Chips, beans and chicken kievs. I couldn't stand this type of food — I was obsessed with feeding the family fresh organic food — but it kept Harry happy. In turn I was happy because I was pleasing him instead of my constant nagging about eating healthy.

"Yesss! Kievs!" Harry cheered as he came rolling into the kitchen.

I turned up the tunes as I began to serve, drum and bass pumping like at most dinner times in our house, except we were buzzing that night because it was a Harry and Lou night in, which meant the kids would go to bed, and mummy and daddy would stay up all night getting smashed.

We laughed and messed around. I ate fast and found myself feeding both kids, even though, at six and two-and-a-half, they should have been able to feed themselves. But we wanted them to get this down quick because we had that Friday feeling.

They're funny, the kids, like angels.

"Bella, Bella! Aren't you a cutie?" Avalon would coo over her baby sister.

Bella would make an Alice Cooper rock face displaying half the contents of her mouth, which always made us belly laugh. For some reason, whatever that child did — no matter how anarchic — she did it with such ridiculous likeability that we fell in love every time. She charmed us all.

I picked up Bella's tiny body and spun her around by the arms. She leaned back, her long messy curls falling behind her. Avalon grabbed around my legs, laughing and dancing, music, music, dancing and laughing.

"Okay, one more tune, kids, then bed," I shouted over the music.

They had pretty good groove, these kids. We were in my office, the room that doubled up as our party room where we'd dance all night. It was also my healing room, aptly named the 'Room of Requirement' by all of our friends. The twinkly lights flashed. I could feel Harry's eyes watching me. I began to flirt with him and then he pointed to his watch with a smile.

"Right, that's it kids. Bedtime!" he said, half-stern half-playful.

"Awwwww, one more, Daddy!" Avalon moaned.

"No, come on. It's bedtime now," he replied, a little shorter than necessary.

"Come on, monkey faces. It's bedtimmmeee," I interjected, turning Bella upside down, and carrying her upstairs. She still felt so tiny.

We tucked the kids into their bunk beds, gave them a million kisses and went through the same routine as always:

"I love you infinity times two."

"I love *you* infinity times 20."

"I love you more than you can ever know."

"I love..."

"Yes, yes, yes. I love you too. Now, go to sleep."

Harry headed downstairs and tidied up the kids' crap that was left around the place. I could hear him washing up the dishes. I didn't know what had got into him in the past year or so. So much had changed. He just did stuff around the house without me having to ask.

I smiled at the thought of our Friday night ritual, as I slipped on my dress and some hold-ups, brushed my hair and applied a little more makeup. I felt the adrenaline running through me. I wandered back into the bedroom, checked the kids, tucked them up. Bella was already flat out on the bottom bunk. I poked my head above the top bunk to see Avalon's eyes sleepy but open.

"You look pretty, Mummy."

"Thank you, darling. I love you."

"Can you do some Reiki on me?"

"Sure, baby."

I put my hands on her head and chest, and swallowed my eagerness to rush this and get downstairs.

"I feel all the angels floating around me, Mummy."

"Me too, baby."

I closed my eyes and felt the energy running from my hands to her little body. I felt the ancientness of her soul, the strength in her, and the innocence of her light. I let my overwhelming love for her, for this Reiki, for my family wash over me.

I heard Harry clinking the dishes downstairs and was torn. So much of me wanted to stay in this energy. For a moment, I realised I didn't want to go downstairs and pollute my body. I noticed my heart felt heavy at the thought of the booze I was about to consume, so I pulled away from my little girl. I didn't want her to feel that.

"Good night, baby. I love you so much."

I put her hands on her heart and tummy.

"Feel the Reiki, baby. Let the angels wash you in golden light and take you to magical places in your dreams. Sleep well. I love you infinity times two."

"Night Mummy. I love you. Will you turn up the music? I like to hear it when I fall asleep."

"Sure, baby."

I shrugged off the heavy heart. I knew I shouldn't do this to my body. I knew it was killing me. But it's what we did! What else would we do to bond? I had to give Harry a little bit of what he needed me to be, as I dragged him along my mystical path.

I headed downstairs. Hearing the clip-clop of my heels on the kitchen floor, Harry turned.

"Alright sexy," he handed me a rum and coke. His eyes were big and excited. I walked over to him, and he grabbed me by the waist and snogged my face.

"You're hot! You're totally gonna get it."

"Come on," I laughed, grabbing my coat off the top of the door, and heading outside for a smoke.

The intensity of our conversation began as it would flow for the rest of the evening. Him not being able to take his eyes off me. Us fully engaged. No phones. No distractions. Just the two of us. We needed this time together.

We talked about how awesome we were as our egos fed from the poisons we put in our body, we poured more rum, smoked more cigarettes, got more trashed. Conversations of what we wanted to do in life, in business. Conversations of what he and I would be doing later in the Room of Requirement, me dancing in my underwear to some dark and sexy tunes.

Evening would flow into morning, when our bellies would hurt from laughing so much, our bodies from all the sex and dancing. And we would creep up to bed praying the kids would sleep in for an extra hour. The path of destruction would make itself visible as it did every Saturday morning. And the consequences of my choices would have me crying in pain with a day-long migraine.

That particular morning, I thought I had the hangover under control by doing Reiki through my body, but eventually the kids came into bed and the pain took over. Avalon climbed in and I rolled over with my back to her. We linked hands and I could feel her protection. She was in mother mode, spooning and healing me. Bella came in soon after and lay between Harry and me. She looked at me. Intuitively, she placed her hand on my forehead and held it there. When I next opened my eyes, she was there still holding my head and looking at me.

My girls. This can't go on. I have to find a new way.

Then came the shame of being a shit mother. It stuck around like a trusty friend as I drifted in and out of my mid-morning sleep.

***

The gateway begins to open

I awoke with something bugging me to look at my phone. I knew what it would be. The defiant teenager in me was refusing to get up to look and my head was so painful that I just wanted to sleep.

Look at your phone.

I knew. I knew what it was going to be. I had been seeing it for weeks and it freaked me out as much as it awakened my curiosity. If I just ignored it, it would go away. I stayed there and let enough time pass for it to have changed, at least five minutes. Then, out of curiosity, I lifted my head from the pillow and checked my phone.

Fuck!

11:11

So much of me wanted to throw the phone across the room. *Leave me alone.* But the other part of me thought, *This is so weird and amazing.*

***

Signs to the sacred ruby

It followed me everywhere from that day. What was it and what did it mean? It was the awakening codes. As soon as we start to awaken to our purpose on earth, the gateway begins to open. No matter how much we resist, no matter how much we sabotage the call with unsociable behaviour, if our soul is ready, our path opens up and the numbers begin to light the way.

I started to see double figures 22, 33, 44. It happened at any moment and every day, sometimes up to 50 times a day. *Angels, you're gonna have to slow this down. I can't read them. I don't know what it all means. If you want my attention, you'll have to send triple figures.* Before I knew it, it was like a computer, numbers everywhere. 1111, 222, 333, 444, 555, 666, 777, 888, 999, 0000, 1234, 4321. Some days I would just see 777, 1111, 444. Other days just 1111. But never a day went by where my head wasn't divinely turned.

I searched the web. Two websites were talking about it back then. I began to read but got the impression that it was down to me to work out my own energetic connection, if only I could find the time.

The summer was so full-on that, when I looked at my diary, the only date that wasn't filled was my birthday. Being out so much meant binge-drinking and abusing my body more than ever. Being good during the week was an attempt to counteract the booze, but on my 34th birthday, I had my greatest lesson in having no expectations and receiving the whole world in your hands. I didn't want to get all our friends out to celebrate my birthday. We had been out every weekend lately. Yet it felt significant enough to do something, so I planned a chilled one. Just catching up with my friend Karina to get her wedding dress altered in London, then going for lunch. The date was set.

On the morning, I woke up and the house was unusually clean and tidy. Everything felt fresh. I walked into the Room of Requirement and on my desk was a float tank voucher. It baffled me.

"Harry, where did you find this?" I asked.

He had no idea what it was.

"But you must have put this here. This is a float tank voucher that I lost last year, but I can't use it because I think I already redeemed it online. Where has it come from?"

Harry just looked at me blankly. I asked Avalon, but she had no idea either. I stared at it. *Weird. Where has this come from?* Then a voice came in. *It's a gift. Take it.*

But isn't that stealing? I reasoned.

It's a gift, Lou. Take it, came the voice.

Floating in saltwater isolation tanks in pure silence and darkness had been something I had done for a few years. They were an expensive treat but I always found them to be a profound space for powerful visions and clarity of the mind. I sensed something wanted me to go. I felt a deep knowing that I would receive a message there.

Fine, fine, I will. But if they notice it's already been redeemed, I'll pay, I decided to myself.

I called the float company and *of course* they had one space left at 10am. I took it and messaged Karina to push back our catch-up. I asked if we could just do lunch. I felt bad because it had been my idea to go out, but she was totally cool about it. Another reassuring sign... I really did need this float!

The city appeared in the train window and the sun hit my face. I wanted to cry with gratitude. I grabbed coffee and lit a cigarette as I walked from Marylebone to Baker Street in a state of utter bliss. Nothing was a rush and everything fell into place. I smiled at anyone who caught my gaze.

A tumbling leaf caught my attention. It floated so gently that it really grabbed my focus. Loud as day, I heard in my ears, *Lou, you are so incredibly blessed.* Tears of gratitude and release stung my eyes as I recognised the enormousness of this long-felt awakening. Emotional, I felt pure peace and joy. *I have the most amazing life. I really do. I bless myself and everyone around me. Life is a most incredible journey.*

On the Tube, I remained peaceful and still. I could feel the energy flowing like a soft blanket. I knew that there was another shift around the corner and what was going on with me right now was big. I felt a detachment and realisation, an opening in myself. I looked up and saw a picture of a rainbow. I smiled, recalling my dreams of rainbows the night before. The sensation deepened my gratitude and awareness — my blissful state hit a new level.

As I sat on the Tube buzzing on this celestial vibe, a lovely looking man got on. He was unthreatening and seemed friendly, almost innocent and sweet. I couldn't help thinking beyond his outward vulnerability. I had a knowing that he was wise, almost angelic. He sat down opposite me. I felt love for him. I smiled and sent him Reiki. When I looked up, he was laughing to himself. He felt it. I knew it. It was a pure oneness moment where I knew he felt the love. It was just so fucking beautiful.

A homeless man got on at the next stop, a cup in his hand. I gave him some coins and blessed him. Then everyone in the carriage got up to give him money one at a time. It was overwhelming. My emotions were rising. It was all too much. I couldn't hold in the pure love and connection I felt around me.

As I walked up the platform at London Bridge, I knew this utter bliss and happiness for all was pure consciousness to a degree. Yes, I'd seen momentary glimpses of it before, but this day I had been in the moment as soon as I'd woken up. This feeling was consistent awareness, which became more and more intense. Utterly overwhelming.

I sat in the station gathering my overflowing emotions. I drank coffee alone, people-watching and crying, crying and people-watching. I had a phone full of birthday messages, and felt so blessed and so held. Every day, I felt increasingly empowered by life's pure essence, as signal after signal from the Universe came my way. As I stepped out of the train station and saw a beautiful orb of light, I took it as yet another message.

Walking to the float tank, I realised this was the first time I had ever been here on my own. I always met Sandy, and after we would wander the streets of London together and talk. A pang of sadness rolled through me. I missed her.

As I handed over my voucher, I prepared myself to have the voucher rejected, but the receptionist simply thanked me and sent me into the small changing room. It smelled damp inside and was dark as a basement. In the centre of the room was the 7-foot long, 6-foot high rounded container that looked like a giant coffin, filled with body-temperature water. As I began to strip off, I was excited to know what would happen. My mind filled with expectation of what this magical call was about to bring. I stepped into the soft salty waters and closed the lid on the world. I lay back. The light dimmed and soft sounds played. Knowing it would be silent within 10 minutes and the music would return 10 minutes before the end, I had 40 minutes of deep uninterrupted stillness of mind, body and soul to spirit-travel and gain wisdom.

My body was awake and my mind still chattering as the music faded. I knew not to force it into stillness. *What we resist persists.* So I relaxed and let my mind do its wandering, trusting that it would soon be engulfed by the stillness and I would take off into Neverland. Time passed and I began berating myself. *Maybe I drank too much coffee beforehand.* But I always had coffee on the way to a float. *What's going on? Why can't I turn off?* My mind became concerned with a sense of failure. A sense that I'd fucked up. My magical moment was going to pass by and I'd never know what it was all about. I contained my thoughts, stayed present and watched them drift by like clouds. I had to accept that I was not going to go deep. Then I had a feeling that something was going to happen at the very end of the experience. I surrendered to the disappointment, let go of what could be, and just observed.

The whale music came on. Time was nearly up. I stayed still in surrender. I had not had a vision. There was nothing I could do but enjoy the last 10 minutes and let my body feel the weightlessness.

Then came the father voice I'd heard in the vision when I was being 'crowned'; the same voice that rang in my ears when I fell to the ground as I was being attacked.

"Go to the antiques market on Old Bond Street and buy your ruby."

I was confused by this comment. After the crowning vision, I had imagined I might get a ruby ring as an heirloom or gift. The instant response in my mind was like a child. *But I thought I was going to be given one?*

The energy was playful, as if rolling its eyes. This made me smile. It felt like a cheeky moment with God. The voice didn't so much speak this time. It was more like a silent filtered reply. Speaking but not speaking. It was telling me, slightly differently, that being handed a ruby was like being given one.

The lights came on and I headed to the shower, going over and over what had just happened. So much of me wanted to rush to get dressed and go tell someone — anyone. But as the waters washed the salt off my body, I began to ground.

I made myself birthday presentable, wearing a short dress and boots. I felt good about myself. I was also pretty bloody pleased with the fact God had just told me to go get my ruby ring.

A state of part-*what-the-fuck?* and part-*of-course*.

***

As I walked towards Borough Market, I soaked in the love of this place. I found myself a seat and lit a cigarette. *Damn this bloody addiction. I can't believe I'm fully smoking again!* Every one of my friends this summer was battling with quitting. I gave myself a break and took out my phone. Karina had texted to say she was two minutes away.

Borough Market was rammed, so we wandered, guided, down a little cobbled street I had never seen before. As I looked up, I was filled with joy at hundreds of umbrellas dangling above us between the buildings. All the restaurants looked busy, but I felt sure we would manifest a table. Sure enough, we asked and one had just become available. But in true Karina style, she wanted one in the sun. I would get a bit embarrassed when she did this, but Karina just strolled over to the busy waiter and asked him to find us a table outside. As the waiter went to say there was nothing, a group of people got up to leave. And there it was; our table.

I wanted to treat Karina. She'd been sick and I needed to look after her and love her. I had been given a few hundred pounds of birthday money and didn't mind spending it on lunch. I told her it was on me. We had two bottles of champagne and a delicious meal in the warm sunshine. My heart filled with love for her, happy she looked well today. I told her all about what had happened in the vision I'd had in the float tank and she didn't seem fazed at all.

"So do you mind if we head to Old Bond Street after lunch and go find this ruby?"

"Sure, we've got loads of time before the gong at 6pm!"

After lunch, I moved out to the courtyard to smoke a cigarette and call Harry. He laughed when I began to tell him.

"So babe, how much can I spend on a ruby?"

"Well, how much do you need for a ruby?"

"I've no idea."

As my mind began to tick over, I did a quick maths calculation in my head and saw that I had spent a fair whack of my birthday money on lunch already. A number popped into my head.

"How about £160?"

"Sure, that's fine. Have a good day. Love you so much. By the way, I'm gonna come meet you in town for a drink later. We'll sort out going for something to eat."

I fucking love Harry so much, I thought grinning.

Both fizzing from the champers, it was 3pm as we headed off to the Tube. I figured we'd just ask someone along the way where this antiques market was, but as we turned onto Old Bond Street, straight ahead was an impressive but weird-shaped Edwardian building on the corner of two streets — Greys Antiques Market. Now, normally, I'd feel out of place in a building like this in the heart of posh Mayfair. As much as I liked to lah-di-dah around drinking champagne, I felt deeply inadequate when it came to old money establishments and would put on a pretence. But today, I strode in and owned it. Today, I had been invited by the heavens. Today, I was chosen and here I was to claim my ruby. Plus, I was a bit pissed!

We walked up the huge steps and entered a labyrinth of tiny shops and stalls. It reminded me of shopping parades and markets in Morocco, but more English and all fancy!

The man told us as we entered that they were starting to close. It was now 4.30pm and they finished at 5pm. I felt an air of confidence. Although more than half the stalls were closing, I sensed that was going to make life easier for me. I looked at the first stall and said assertively, "I'm looking for a ruby."

The man pulled out a tray about a metre-squared from a display cabinet. It held various ruby rings, but even before I saw the prices started around £5000, I didn't vibe with them. *Thank God!* I walked on, more confident now I had an idea of what a ruby looked like! I realised I had never even seen one before. The next stall was closed, then a beautiful blonde lady in maybe her late forties greeted us at the next. When she smiled, I was thrown at how welcoming she was. She was so elegant that I was convinced she would see I didn't belong here. I smiled back and looked into her jewellery cabinet where I saw the most glorious ruby ring, surrounded with diamonds.

"Wow! Can I look at that, please?"

She willingly took out the ring and I placed it on my finger. It was utterly lovely. This was the ring I wanted. It felt majestic, stunning.

"How much is this?" I asked.

"That one is £23,000," she replied.

I laughed out loud.

"Maybe for my 35th!"

It was a relief to not pretend I could afford it. I kept it on for a few moments, wondering if I could manifest it for next year. Then I gave it back and Karina chipped in.

"We're looking for something more around the couple of hundred pounds mark."

A pang of shame washed over me, but Karina had always done this. She had no judgment and thought everyone else was like that too, so she was never afraid to ask. I'd always loved and hated that about her, because she always got what she wanted without shame, but it triggered all of my own. The woman replied in a genuine and non-judgmental tone, matching Karina's.

"Rubies are semi-precious stones. You're very unlikely to get one for that price."

"I have to find one. I've been told there is one here for me. It's definitely here."

I could sense she liked me and wanted to help, as though some part of her knew how much I needed this. She recognised how impossible it was but wanted to search for an answer too.

Without questioning my bizarre reaction, she replied, "Well, there's a lady over the other side who is still open. You could try her. She sells much cheaper jewellery."

I was already off, looking back and beaming a thank you over my shoulder. We reached the stall run by an older lady with hair pinned on top of her head and half-moon glasses. She looked like she should have been in the theatre. As we approached, she was serving another man, but she looked up and smiled.

"I'm looking for a ruby ring for £160. Do you have anything? I was sent here by a spiritual message to come buy it."

She looked unfazed by what I said, excused herself from the man, leaving him looking at the watches, and pulled out a ruby that looked just like the one in the vision, but huge. *Wow, this is it!*

"This is £800, but it's man-made, so it's not a real ruby as such."

My heart sunk but I started bargaining with myself. *Maybe I just need to buy this. This is the one.* But there was a part of me that was also disappointed, especially as I would have to go into debt for this one and it wasn't a true ruby. Karina, from the far end of the counter, lifted her head. She was pointing at something.

"What's that?"

The lady walked over and pulled out the teeniest little gold ring, high crown setting, with a tiny ruby. Instantly, I thought, *That's a bit small.*

"How much is it?" Karina asked.

The woman looked at the sticky label. Adjusting her eyes as she peered down over her glasses as if to inspect the ring, she gasped.

"One hundred and sixty-five pounds."

She was taken aback, but I laughed. I wasn't even shocked. In a flippant air of knowing, I said, "Let's see if it fits, shall we?"

I placed it on the middle finger of my left hand and it fitted perfectly. I felt like Cinderella! By now, even the man looking at the watches was staring in shock, while Karina looked on, pretty damn pleased with herself, but also with a sense of expectation we can all learn from.

"Can I pay by card?"

She hesitated, "We don't really take cards."

"I don't have any cash on me," I replied.

"You can go and get cash from the cash point. It's just over the road, at the top of Bond Street."

I didn't want to leave this miracle bubble and I didn't want to leave this building without the ring. It was nearly 5pm, everywhere was closing, and I couldn't be arsed to go and come back.

"If you have a card machine, can't we just use it?" I asked.

"If we use the machine, I can't make you a deal."

"What deal would you normally make?"

"I would probably take off £10," the lady said.

"How about we meet halfway? If you take off just £5 but use my card..."

She called her boss downstairs and he agreed. And I walked out with my ruby for exactly £160.

I was in a daze on the Tube staring down at the ring on my finger. My head was spinning with downloads that I simply couldn't process. It was as if a gateway had opened up and the wisdom of the earth was flowing through me like a river, but it was flowing so fast I couldn't catch all the whispers. I really had been chosen, just like the vision I had had all those months ago had said!

***

Avalon looked blissful in the back of the car, gazing out the window.

"What's going on in your mind, baby girl?" I asked her.

"I love the way music makes me feel. This one makes me feel like I'm running through golden fields with Bella. It makes me think how sad and happy life is. It makes me think of a life without you in it, and I don't want that, but I know you're an angel and you'll always be here to watch over me. And you've taught me to be an angel, too."

My heart back-flipped. I didn't want to die young, but there was this fear still inside that I would and she could read it. Avalon could read everything in me. She was telepathic and she could predict the future too, which I hoped this was not. She was a connected intuitive being of light.

And so, I needed to heal this fear of mine. I knew it would only happen by stepping up and doing what I was here to do on earth. Now I had clarity, even though it scared me, I would properly finish up with my funeral business, and let go of my obsession with death and dying.

I had to start teaching Reiki.

No sooner had I made this declaration to myself than a message came. *Call Peter at the woodland burial ground.* It was a sacred place for me. I loved the timber-framed, glass-fronted gathering hall that looked out onto the vast woodland where many rested. As Peter and I wandered the grounds catching up, I told him all about the signs I'd been seeing and that I was closing my business.

"I'm going to teach Reiki."

Immediately, Peter suggested that I went and taught there in the gathering hall.

"This woodland is your home. It's part of you. Come teach here. We'll support you as you grow!"

I cried and thanked Peter, silently sending up gratitude to the angels too.

"Yes please! I'd love that."

Oh shit, this is really going to happen then.

***

The sacred opal

As with any major change in my life, Glastonbury began to call me home. The lands of my soul whispered in my dreams, *Root to the earth, Lou. Come home.*

Driving down the lanes to Glastonbury, the sun shone bright and the world looked sepia-toned. My life was a dream. I leaned my arm out the window, Jimi Hendrix's *Angel* playing to my soul, and processed the conversations I'd been having with Harry lately about our true essence and power centres. The ring had seemingly stirred some acceptance of my spirituality in him, and although it wavered still and sometimes annoyed him, today he was remarkably open.

I'd recounted some of my visions from my meditations to Harry, especially the grids and shapes I would see but didn't yet understand. He listened, even asking questions. In some ways, he was so wise and conscious, and I began to honour his need to seek a scientific understanding of my experiences. We were forming a bridge, where science and spirituality met. We agreed maybe science just didn't have the answers yet! Even Avalon got involved, when the topic turned to metaphysics.

Harry could feel what I was feeling. Tears rolled down my cheeks knowing he believed in me. The number sequences were so alive in our lives, especially on journeys like this one, when even he and the girls would see them — 1111, 222, 777, 888, 1234, following us, on car registrations, the car mileage, in emails, on clocks. There was no denying the divine.

We reached Glastonbury in time to have a wander.

"I think we're going to find the opal from my dream," I said, referencing a recent vision I'd relayed to Harry.

I had never seen him so willing to explore the crystal shops.

"Who the fuck are you, Harry?" I joked, "You'll be growing a beard next and waving your own wand."

"I can always go to the pub and wait for you!" he laughed.

But I liked him being comfortable in the hippiness of it all. Today, there was nothing that felt like the right stone, so I let it go.

That night, I attuned Avalon to her Reiki 2 level. It was beautiful. At the end, she looked at me with her big brown eyes and took a breath.

"Thank you, Mummy," she said, tears rolling down her cheeks, "You're amazing. I'm so proud you're my mummy."

The dark night of the new moon gave me a deep connection to the mystic. I gave thanks to the Universe for my family and life, and sent love, peace and understanding to everyone as I drifted off to sleep. I awoke the next morning more refreshed than I had been in a long time.

"Harry, I know what we need to do to manifest this opal from my vision. We need to set a number in our mind and then it will come to us! I reckon it will be £50. Does that feel okay with you?"

"Let's do it," he replied.

His eagerness to join me on this mission was almost more exciting than the prospect of the stone.

Later that morning, we walked back to the crystal shop on the corner where we'd been the day before.

"I'm looking for a polished opal about £50."

"I have one," the old man said, ducking into the back room, and coming back with a tiny opal.

"That's it!" I cried.

It was £60. I tried to negotiate him down to £50. *This is the one.* I knew it was right as I held it in my hands.

"I can give it to you for £53 but that's my best price."

"I'll take it," I said.

Harry looked proud and the kids were excited.

"You've got more magic now, Mummy!"

I laughed. She was right.

"Let's all go to the sacred springs and get even more magical."

I was practised by now at hiding my surprise when Harry agreed. We set off and reached the springs via a dark cold cave under the Glastonbury Tor. The brick walls that created the pool were lit with rows and rows of candles. At the far end of the pool was an altar. It felt sacred, because it was sacred.

I followed the dark brick steps to an even deeper pool at the far corner of the cave. I pulled off my clothes, not caring who was in there, and put my foot in the freezing water. Harry didn't flinch at what would normally be too far out for him. All he did was stand there, allowing me space to do what I needed to do.

"Mummy, are you really going in naked?" the girls laughed as they also began to strip off.

I walked along the slippery walls to the plunge pool, where the 'guardian of the cave' helped me up the steps. I didn't care that he could see me; we were in sacred waters, here to be purified. Someone began singing, beautiful sounds filling my heart, and the sound echoing around the walls. I stood at the water's edge and said a prayer.

I am in service to you. By the grace of God and all my guides who love me unconditionally, wash me free and assist me in my soul purpose here on the earth.

I jumped in, the cold hitting my entire body. This was my own baptism, my commitment to my soul's purpose here on earth.

Shaking from the cold, I beamed an exhilarated smile to Harry. I could hear the kids' laughter echoing around the cave. They were in their knickers in the lower pool. I observed how confident Avalon was in this environment and watched as she waded through the water, taking her little sister along with her. And as she passed the altar, she bowed.

The message was undeniable. I was already living my purpose. Raising conscious contented kids.

***

Call to service

Random messages came in thanking me for just being me. *Must be the full moon,* I thought to myself.

"Lou, I know we don't really know each other, but I read your posts on Facebook every day. They help me feel better about the world. I thought you should know."

"Lou, I need to thank you. Profound shifts have happened since our session. You are my angel. Thank you."

"Lou, credit where credit is due. I felt it was time to tell you how you've changed my life…"

Six different people sent me random messages that day, thanking me for changing their lives in some way. It was too much to take. I was still learning how to receive compliments and see my own value. I remembered the message from Jesus the summer before that I must learn to be comfortable with people looking up to me. Still, I felt awkward.

Not knowing what to do with myself, I pulled out my laptop and began to type, just to release the discomfort inside me. But there was no getting away from it. Something was typing the messages through me…

Lou, you are ready to do your work. You cannot delay your calling. You have had all the assurance you need that you are ready for this work. You have proven to yourself that you have a gift and a power that is to be shared and taught to others.

There were none of my usual dyslexic typos or bad spelling. It was a clear message from somewhere beyond myself.

* * *

The next day was the long-awaited wedding of our best friends Mark and Karina. Over the day, I would find quiet times to sit back and observe all these people I loved so much. We were like family. We had all grown together and now our kids were growing together. I knew everything was changing inside of me. I wasn't going to be what they knew me to be anymore. I felt a pang of sadness.

The summer nights were getting cooler. And something else, not just summer, was drawing to an end. I was saying goodbye to a part of my life I had loved. It was time to prepare for the new chapter.

I'd always loved September. It brought new choices, new challenges, new dreams, stepping away from what had become comfortable in life — habits, crutches, addictions — and stepping towards being a teacher of the energy. I was just two weeks away from teaching my first class.

CHAPTER 11

UNDERGRADUATE OF REBIRTH

Path of the wounded healer

TEACHING REIKI AND conscious awareness came completely naturally in the end. I had falsely doubted myself. I *was* a good teacher. I watched as my students did their own personal work, healing their own pain and transforming into human angels. Their awakenings were truly magical and rewarding to witness.

Dare to enter the cave of despair and darkness to meet your deepest wound and face your greatest fear and meet your darkest shadow. The path to enlightenment is destructive, yet holds opportunities to alchemise your wounds into wisdom and your pain into power.

Come deep into the belly of the mother earth, become primal in your release. Allow yourself to sit in this darkness for a while, until you uncover the roots of the pain: from this lifetime, or many lifetimes ago. Honour this space. This is exactly where you need to be.

In the darkness there is always a light. Look for it. Call upon it to shine on what you need to see so you can peel off those old layers of crap that have been hiding your inner light — freeing your soul from unnecessary attachments so you are ready to rebirth back into the world. A lighter, wiser, awakened version of you.

***

I stepped outside into the garden and noticed a huge bird under a bush. I had never seen such a thing. I sat on the doorstep and peered at it. It didn't move, but it was alive. It was quite an ugly-looking bird from where I sat 10 feet away. Then I realised... it was a heron!

Yet again, I'd seen four in one week in totally different places. Considering they were a rare sighting in my world, I had begun to pay attention. Maybe this was my animal totem, or some kind of spirit messenger.

I went to the supermarket and bought some fish to see if I could feed it. It refused the food. I sat close to it for hours, beaming Reiki. It didn't move. I prayed for him. Still nothing! *Poor broken heron, why have you chosen my garden to land? What are you showing me?*

By sunset, I realised he wasn't going to fly and needed help. I called the RSPB and they confirmed he had broken his leg. I cried when they took him away, feeling guilty. *He needed fixing and I couldn't fix him. He came to deliver a message. I couldn't even understand it and now he's gone!*

***

Dark night of the soul

Something drew me into my cave that night. For months, I'd had a constant pain behind my right ear. It felt like something was growing there and now the pressure was hard to ignore. I felt a stirring inside too. *Maybe it's all the teaching I'm doing bringing up some weird stuff.*

I thought everyone who had young girls had the same fear. I would lie awake at night, flashing horror scenes in my mind: men trapping the girls in a room; the girls being taken and raped; the girls hiding in a corner, fearful and broken. I didn't *want* to worry about it. And the older Avalon and Bella got, the more I realised I wouldn't always be around to protect them from the baddies in the world. *You simply can't protect the girls all the time,* I kept telling myself. *What if someone did come and take them? They have Reiki. They could heal themselves and communicate with me through the energy. I could find them. I would find them.*

Nonetheless, fear gripped me. Normally, I never watched the news, because it had a terrible effect on me, but I was an avid player on social media and would see articles about paedophile rings and abused children that broke my heart. I prayed for the freedom of all children and sent Reiki healing to them wherever they were.

Harry refused to listen to me go on about it. He'd walk away or change the subject.

"Lou, you need to stop reading that stuff. You know the world is not all bad. All we can do is bring them up to be strong and brave and to trust their intuition."

Harry was right. I knew the power of thought. I had to think about what I *wanted* for them, and not what I *feared* for them. "Dream the world you wish into being," as the saying went.

Thoughts of the girls being joyful and safe brought me peace.

***

Harry kissed me, his hand gliding down between my legs. I froze, fear gripping my body. I couldn't breathe. *Fuck! What is happening to me?* I didn't want to reject him, so I stayed where I was, as still as a mannequin.

"What's up?" he said.

"I don't know," I replied.

"Lou?"

I could feel it. I closed down. I rolled over, holding my belly, tears flowing from nowhere.

"Lou, what's wrong?"

"I don't know, I don't know," I sobbed.

He tugged on my shoulder to get me to face him.

"Babe, what's wrong?"

"I don't know, I don't know, I don't know, I don't know, I don't know."

The words fell out one after the other, like a broken record, stuck, trapped on a loop. Harry pulled me close and I sobbed into his chest. Much of me wanted to run. Another part of me wanted to stay safe in his arms.

"Shhh." He held me like a baby, rocking me, kissing the top of my head. I sobbed uncontrollably.

"What's going on, babe? Did I do something?"

"No, no, not you," I managed, taking a breath.

I sat up with my knees to my chest. Harry turned on the side light.

"Something weird is happening. Everything is crumbling. Whatever has been trying to raise its head has risen. Something's triggered me. It started a few years ago when I went to that healer women with the coloured bottles, and memories and fears came up from when I was little. I tried to ignore it at the time, but now I'm obsessed with Avalon being taken, fearful something may happen to her. I'm aware now that I was desperate to learn Reiki so I could teach the kids, in case they were ever *taken* by a paedophile! In my head, I thought maybe if they knew Reiki, they could use it to heal themselves, use the magic to escape and connect with me. I've never questioned why I would think such a thing, but I'm starting to see it. Memories keep coming to me, memories, strange memories. Being in a hotel room with a man, an old man. I was so young. So, so young."

Harry didn't say a word. He just held me even closer. As if he could squeeze me and it would all go away. I fell asleep sobbing on his chest and woke up in the middle of the night. I must have unconsciously been healing myself in my sleep, as I could feel the energy flowing around my body.

In my half-conscious haze, I heard my outer-self talking to my body-self. I could hear a voice, which was mine, but also sounded soothing and Scottish. Like I was my own guardian angel. I had no idea what she was saying, but there were constant whispers. I called upon Angel Gabriel. I felt myself asking to be a child of his light and to channel the message clearly. Here he was again, gently warming me.

I heard a noise in the house, like a pinging on the metal of the lamp in the spare room. Then it happened on the lamp next to me in the bedroom. Then the same sound rang in my own head, shockingly loudly. I sent distance Reiki to the girls straight away. For the first time ever, I felt scared in my own house, as if a darker energy was there. Then I remembered my own fear would create a darker energy, so I faced the fear and tried to disperse it.

The energy felt sinister. I closed my eyes. Reiki flowed and I began to journey into another world, a dark and terrifying world, though I refused to be scared by the visions. I was almost flying, trying to be brave. I had the power to change the fear, so I embraced it, truly felt it, and it shifted.

Next, some words came to me.

Even though I walk through the valley of the shadow of death, I will fear no evil, for you are with me. Your rod and your staff, they comfort me.

The Bible? I didn't even realise I knew any Bible verses.

At the end of the vision, a man in a black cloak offered me a sapphire ring. I wasn't sure if I should take it as I couldn't be certain it wasn't evil, but I took it, knowing it was only fear. I understood that this ring was representative of another level. At some point, I would receive a sapphire when I was ready to live that level.

The next day I dropped Bella at nursery and took myself off to the river to process what was coming up for me. The more I walked and listened to that inner guide, the more I felt a wisdom from deep inside. *Something did happen to me when I was little.* Even admitting that to myself stirred something inside me that made me want to run. I had to go home and do some Reiki on myself. I had to understand more.

That afternoon I lay my hands on my body and felt a release of dead energy. With tears streaming down my cheeks, I let the stillness of the Reiki wash through me. I knew there was somewhere I had to go. Something had happened to me that day. I began to travel back in time...

There wasn't a hopscotch near the poolside, so I made my own game, jumping over the lines. It was bad luck to step on a line, so I paid particular attention. I never walked over three drains either. Two drains was okay, but three was unlucky.

No-one was around. The hotel was so quiet. Maybe it was early morning and nobody had come down yet or maybe it was off-season.

I hopped faster over the paving stones, past the little swimming pool, past the hedges towards the big swimming pool. I saw a couple on the sun loungers. They looked old, but not as old as my nanny and grandad. They started talking to me, but I couldn't fully understand their broken German accents.

I wanted to be a good girl and try to speak back to them. They asked if I was allowed to play on my own by the pool. They asked where my parents were. I told them they were in the room. They began to get their things, their towels, their bag and they took my hand.

"Come for cake."

"I'm not allowed to go anywhere else," I said.

I was polite, because that's the sort of child I was. It took bravery to speak up. They started speaking to me in a way I didn't understand.

"You can come with us. It's okay."

"Mummy said I have to stay by the pool."

I was trying not to be rude, but they had me by the hand. I was being led away from where I had been playing towards the main hotel. I was scared and said again that I had to go back or my mum would be cross, but I couldn't seem to make them understand that I wasn't allowed to go with them. They ignored me and walked me towards the stairs.

"I want to go back now," I said.

The next memory came. It was fear. I was upstairs in a strange hotel room. There was a small table, a chair, twin beds. They told me to sit on the chair. I obeyed. The woman stood by the sliding doors looking out. The man reached for a bottle on top of a cupboard.

"I want to go home now. My mummy and daddy will be cross with me," I said again.

He replied, "We're just going to have a drink and then we can go."

He poured me a drink. I smelled it. It was alcohol. I knew the smell, even at four years old. My nanny and grandad had this drink. The only alcohol I was allowed to try was the 'yellow stuff' at Christmas. I could run my finger around my nan's empty glass and taste the Advocaat. But this wasn't yellow stuff. It smelt strong and I knew I wasn't allowed it. I was scared. I wanted to go back. They wouldn't let me.

I couldn't see any more images from the scene in the room. I had no memory after that. Just a feeling that I needed to be nice to them so they would let me go. Then a feeling of relief that I was allowed out, which must have been some time later, because the next image I recall was the door opening to the hotel lobby and all this commotion...

Dad leaping for the man...

Police pulling him back...

Being scared Dad was going to get into trouble...

And nothing more.

***

The night after the dark night

That evening I sat on our bed and told Harry what had come up. I felt like I was making it all up and was ashamed even talking about it. Harry listened as he folded the clothes, not saying much. I could feel he was uncomfortable. He didn't know what to say. I sensed I needed to save him from this moment, so abruptly I ended the conversation.

"Shall I make you a cup of tea?" I said lightly, almost joyfully, breaking the moment like a hammer to glass.

"That would be great," he said, as if we'd been chatting about decorating the house.

I walked downstairs pained, rejection flowing through my veins, pumping through my heart, mind-fucking thoughts, then anger. *Why didn't he hug me? I needed him to wrap his arms around me and make it all better.* As the kettle boiled, I fell into despair. *He thinks I'm disgusting. I'm used. I'm dirty.* I felt disgusting.

Harry came downstairs and sat at the computer in the Room of Requirement. I walked in, hoping he would give me something, anything. Placing down the tea, moving deliberately, creating an opportunity for him to save me from my mind-fuck. He was off in another world looking at football results as if the world just went on as normal. Masking my hurt, I went back upstairs to the bedroom, holding the wall as I tried to catch my breath, looking around for something to help me as the rising pain began to choke me. I was turning into a child. I needed my mum. I needed someone. I climbed into my floor-to-ceiling wardrobe, pulled the door across, and rocked and rocked, trying to silence my tears while the other part of me looked on in bemusement thinking, *What the fuck are you doing, Lou? Sort it out.*

I sobbed and sobbed until I stood back up. I watched myself walk back down the stairs, in a daze, looking to stop this, looking for my normal world again. I stood at the door of the office, like a child looking for attention.

"Harry, do you think I'm disgusting? Are you ashamed of me?"

He turned around, his eyes furious.

"How fucking dare you accuse me of thinking such a thing?"

I began to shake violently, shocked at his response. From the sidelines, I saw myself fall to my knees, raise my arms in the air, and begin to scream and howl. Everything happened in slow motion. I watched his eyes look at me with fury, disgust at my behaviour. He was saying something I couldn't hear.

As this turmoil was going on, my soul observed Harry's soul out of his body.

You just need to pick me, Harry, I'm suffering, it went.

Then our two souls stepped back into our bodies. There was noise. There was pain. Time returned to full speed.

Harry scooped me up from the ground and I wrapped my legs around him like a baby. Our hearts pressed against each other, I began to catch my breath between sobs. I calmed down as he stroked my hair and wiped my eyes. We said nothing. Peace began to flow around us. I could touch my normal life again. Harry carried me into the kitchen and sat me on the worktop looking into my eyes.

"Lou, I think we need to get you some help, maybe take you to Harley Street or something."

It was such a weird thing to hear him say. Where had this come from? Fear rolled through me, imagining the drugs they'd put me on to shut me down and keep me quiet.

"No," I said firmly but softly, "I can heal this myself. I can do this. I know I can."

"Lou, this abuse stuff breaks my heart. I wish there was more I could do to help. I wish I knew the answers to give you, but I just don't. I can't help and that frustrates me to the point where I want to explode, but I have no experience of anything like this. All I can offer you is a cuddle and love, which is always there for you."

"I can heal this myself. I can do this with Reiki."

He looked at me with soft eyes trying to gauge if he was looking at the Lou who had just broken down or the Lou he knew. I saw relief and knew Harley Street wasn't the path he wanted for me either but had been the only solution he knew.

"If you're sure, babe."

I felt it in my bones.

"I know I can. I just need to know you're okay to let me cry and be a bit mental occasionally!"

He took my face in his hands and kissed me on the forehead.

"We'll get through it."

***

What do I need to heal this?

It was a cold late October morning and the final leaves were falling from the trees. I knew this season so well. I could feel the earth's beating heart under my feet. I could feel her calling me to come back home so she could hold me on her belly, rooting me enough to withstand the winds she was going to send to blow the dead leaves from my soul. She was preparing me for my own winter. She was sending me to my inner cave where I had no choice but to face the darkness.

I found myself driving to the river again after the school run. The fog was heavy, not a dog-walker in sight; just me wandering through the thickness of this mystical haze. I made my way to my favourite seat, a memorial bench for a lady called June, who knew all my years of worries. Returning to this place was like curling up in the comfort of my grandmother's lap.

Headphones in and hood over my head, I put my feet up and laid back. Naturally, I placed one hand on my chest, one on my belly. I began sobbing to the music. London Grammar played into my heart; that voice alone was enough to help me feel my lifetime of suppressed pain. An hour must have passed lying there, tears warming my face. I began to feel a release and a sense of peace. As I opened my eyes, between the mist and the clouds, a golden stream of light broke through right onto my forehead. I was being blessed. It was magical.

What do I need to heal this? I asked the light. I waited for the answer. I couldn't talk to my mum. I had tried to speak with her about it, but it was too hard. I didn't want to upset her. I didn't want to make a big deal out of it. Then I had a deep urge to call my dad.

It was over three years since we'd spoken. It went to voicemail, as I knew it would. In my mind, he only came back into my life when something had gone wrong with his latest girlfriend and he had no-one else to chat to.

"Dad, it's Lou. Sorry to bother you but I need help with something. I need to know what happened to me when we were on holiday when I was little and that couple took me. Some stuff is coming up."

He rang back within minutes and I was shocked to get such a quick response.

"Hi Dad?" I said cagily.

"Lou, I don't know what happens to abused children later on in life, so I don't know what you're going through, but I'll do what I can to help you with what I know."

Like being hit with a stick, that was unexpected. He hadn't hesitated. I'd never known my dad so direct, so open, so willing to discuss anything. This was certainly a revelation. I was even more taken aback with his openness than by what he'd said. I had no words.

"I don't know what happened, Lou. All I can do is answer your questions," he said.

His voice was matter-of-fact, but warm. I remembered that I loved him. Even missed him. Recalling the reasons I am who I am because of him, despite our turbulent hot-and-cold relationship, he was a good human. He was doing the best he could and always had. He was the reason I loved music. He'd taught me about the culture like no-one else had, ensuing that I had fully understood the deeper meaning of Marvin Gaye's 'What's Going On' album. I loved him despite our disconnect. I took a deep breath, not knowing how to be with this new energy between us.

"How long was I gone for, Dad?"

"An hour, maybe two," he said with sense of surrender to his own pain, "I can't remember exactly to be honest, Lou."

There was a sincerity that I had not heard from him in a long while.

"What was I like when they brought me back?"

"Lou, your mum was so mad with you when you came down the stairs. She shouted and it upset you. I didn't see what your face was like before that, so I don't know."

I sensed something wasn't quite right with that statement, almost a passing or denying of responsibility. But there was both truth and untruth in what he had said. He had spent his life lying to me. It was just normal for him. But I'd always been able to see through it. I knew if I challenged him he would hang up, close down on me. I had to tread carefully if I wanted to keep this connection between us open.

I remembered the doors opening, seeing police, and being upset because I thought Dad was going to get in trouble for launching at the man who was by my side. I supposed there were different versions of the story. It was over 30 years ago and I'd already accepted I would never know the truth. Mum had told me I was gone for 10 minutes and was fine. Dad had told me I was gone for maybe two hours. I had no memory after the man tried to give me alcohol. I kept thinking it was all an elaborate drama that I had created in my head.

Maybe I should stop digging.

***

That weekend, I went to my mum's and I broached the subject with her.

"Lou, I came to find you and you had gone."

I felt the horror my mum would have felt. My heart burned, imagining what it would be like to lose one of the girls now.

"I looked everywhere for you. I told the hotel to call the police, but they wouldn't do it. It was an hour before they would get the police involved."

I didn't want to hear anymore nor for her to suffer. I reassured her that she was an amazing mum. I wanted to forget about it. I wanted it to go away. I wanted to just drink wine together and chat about something else.

But I couldn't help thinking about the parents in the world whose children went missing. It twisted me up to imagine the pain and suffering. It was unimaginable to think of all the children that never came home. *Don't go into those thoughts. They don't serve you. They're a dark hole you do not need to travel down,* I told myself.

The following week, it came up more and more. And the throbbing behind my right ear became more pronounced. I put away the nagging feeling that it may be a growth or tumour. After all, I didn't have any of the symptoms according to Google. But I knew there was something there that shouldn't be. I was more tired than normal. I wasn't my usual self, dancing around the house being playful. I didn't want to see any clients, and sure enough, the Universe heard my wish and one by one my clients sent texts saying that they couldn't make their appointments. I loved how that worked. Manifesting at its best. I didn't even need to do anything.

I took it as a sign to go back to bed and rest, putting aside any guilt that it was a Monday morning.

As I passed my desk on the way up to bed, I felt guided to take with me a black stone that was lying there. It was an apache tear stone that an old friend of Harry's had sent me as a thank you for helping her. The note that had come with it said, "I'm not into this stuff, but I found this in a shop and had an overwhelming urge to send it to you."

I got into bed, placed the stone on my heart, put my hands on my belly. The Reiki began to flow. My third eye was pulsating. I felt angels all around me, then the most wonderful maternal energy came close. She stroked my forehead.

"You are safe," she spoke.

Angels held my hands as I saw myself walking down pathways of golden light. I was little again and I was scared. Then I was my own angel, the grown-up Lou taking the tiny hand of little Louise. I was there on the chair again. He wanted me to drink this alcohol.

I whispered into the ears of my child self, "I am looking over you, little one."

I began to see something. I was lying down. I could see his face. He wanted me to do something. I shot up, waking myself from the journey and screaming from the base of my belly.

"I don't want to see it, I don't want to see it, I don't want to see it."

I sat bolt upright, panting, sweating, fully back in my bedroom, feeling the sweat dripping down my body. I rolled over and stared at the wall.

The angel was still there. She stroked my head again, calming me, soothing me.

"It's okay. You don't need to."

***

The pains of the past were alive in me still, and weeks after the conversation with my dad, I was still heavy. I couldn't seem to shift it. I closed down sexually with Harry, which was having an impact on us. I sought comfort in my spirituality, spending hours consulting my oracle cards, rather than talking. Meditating more and cuddling less. Communicating with my guides, not seeking solace in him.

I need to create peace with my past before I can create peace in my future. I feel alone myself. It must be hard for Harry. I am changing so fast, and even though I am still me, there are parts of me he cannot reach. For a while, we were the same frequency, but I moved on.

I didn't speak to anyone about it. No one could help me. I had to be the one to navigate my way out of this. My journal became my mentor. I mastered communication with my spirit guides, writing without the mind, letting messages come through on the page without involving the ego. I meditated and asked for rituals to help me move forward. I was given the answer as my pen moved across the page...

There will be a time. This time will come in the most random of hour. You must wake and light the green candle. Look into the flame and ask your heart to forgive and let go of all that no longer serves you. Allow the green light to come though you and then look into that beautiful green light and you will see a future of your destiny.

Letting go, it will be hard to detach from the material. It will be one of your hardest elements to free. But you will see that there is a greatness ahead that will imprint your mind and drive you further than you have ever been before. Your fears of being unable to complete anything will go, along with the emotional attachments to the necessary.

Use this time with the turquoise stone that was sent to you last week. Place it between your legs as you sit on a cushion, a blanket draped around your shoulders. When you have seen the vision, you must let the candle burn out, and lie there until it has gone.

There will be pain. There will be emptiness within. You will bear scars. They will heal. But the insight will be more powerful than you have ever known. You have a power within to communicate this with the world.

***

Soundtrack to self-healing

I was struggling with migraines. I took myself off for yet another afternoon nap, this time not hiding my tears from Harry, who was in turmoil knowing what to do with me.

When I awoke an hour or so later, I felt Harry sitting behind me cross-legged, one hand between my shoulders, one hand at the base of my back. He was giving me Reiki! Tears fell out of pure love for him. I lay there not speaking, just feeling the energy coming from his hands into my body. Receiving his healing.

"Thank you, thank you, thank you," I whispered.

"I didn't know what else to do," he said back.

It was more than I ever could have expected. My big strong man of science, healing me like this. I rolled over and hugged him so tight. We made love slowly, healing in every move.

That evening Harry offered to put the kids to bed, so I could go upstairs and do more healing. I raided my crystal collection and placed my apache tear stone, greenstone and snowflake obsidian on my heart, solar plexus and sacral chakras. Something in me knew this self-Reiki session was going to be a mad one; I was nervous. With all I had been through these past few weeks, I just wanted to be whole again.

Unconsciously, I'd compiled a playlist that day, not realising it was about to become the soundtrack to the biggest self-healing of my life. Deep beats, dark beats, down-tempo hypnotic electronic beats, mixed with piano, cinematic sounds that would help me journey to parts of the soul that needed to be held.

I lay my hands on the front of my sacral area, fingers pointing down almost in a triangle around my second chakra, a portal to my womb. I asked in my conscious mind for the angels to help me heal. Then my subconscious voice took over, prayer words coming from a deeper place.

Please heal my heart. I am fully committed to going where I need to go. I understand that this will cause pain and I am ready to accept the pain that this will bring. I am ready to be free so I can fly with my purpose and be the best I can be.

Dear God, Jesus, all my angels, be with me now as I take my final leaps, and jump into freedom and trust within myself. Be with me and hold my hands. Make your presence known so I can feel you with clarity and be fully connected. Please heal my heart, so I can be light again.

Even though my hands were nowhere near it, my heart area warmed. All the way down, my left side filled with white light. A montage of images came to me: pain, flashbacks, wounded times.

Then a message from a deep knowing, *Music is spirit herself. This is why you connect to music. You feel her and she feels you. She is the sounds in your ears every day, guiding you, filling you with love and hope.*

Now I was looking into a gaping hole in my stomach. I couldn't understand this void. This is where I felt sadness for myself. I didn't want to feel it, but I had to stand here and face it. I felt stuck in this place.

An angel spoke, *You must learn what you truly want in your life. The boundaries and relationships you allow into your life affect your energy. Protect your energy so you can move forward to recreate your life standing in your own power.*

I could see that freedom came in a new way of thinking and being. My stomach hurt. My heart hurt. Tears screamed to escape, but I pushed them down.

Then I felt the pain in my head, like a dark tumour. There was searing heat and a hand stroking my face to reassure me. For now, the tumour in the back of my head was real, a dark mass that had been controlling me, an entity. It came to me from him, from that man, feeding off the pain from my dad, off all the energy of all the times I'd been disempowered in my life, off everyone who had pulled my strings. I'd been available for everyone to feed from my energy.

The mass got hotter and hotter. The flashbacks began. All the times I had allowed myself to be used, all the rejection, all the men from my past who had used my body, their seeds contaminating my soul. *To be free, I must forgive. To forgive, I must cut cords and connections, conscious or unconscious, from this life and others.*

Physical and emotional pain burned and rose to the surface. All the pain of all the women in all the world who had ever felt the same rose within me too. I was healing not just for me, but for every woman, for my ancestors, for my sisters. *I must forgive, let go, everyone, everything, clear, clear, clear.*

Everything went black. I went in and out of different dimensions. I was not in control of anything. Something had taken over my body and my soul. All I could feel was the emptiness in my belly.

An angel spoke again, *You must love you. Fill that void with love for you.*

Then darkness came. I was paralysed. I felt caged. A single tear fell. The energy was intense, as though the mass in my head was a black hole sucking everything from me, *Oh God, I'm going to die.* Time gathered around me. The pain was too much, more than anything I had ever known. *My head is going to implode. This is it.* Death was here. This was my time. I could do nothing, so I surrendered, accepting this was my time.

I heard the TV downstairs. The real world slipped through the veils of the invisible world for a moment, reminding me life in the house went on. Life would go on without me. The tumour imploded. Pain seared through from my head to my entire body. *I'm going to die.*

White light settled all around me, but I wasn't dead. The black hole had not sucked in my life.

That is enough now, whispered the angels.

The music stopped. The playlist had come to an end.

As I lay there, dumbfounded and shocked to my core, the sounds of normal life returned. I could hear Harry downstairs in the kitchen. I felt sensitive. I dared not move my head.

Instead, I smiled and stayed in the stillness, happy to be alive.

And, at last, out of the deep dark cave.

***

CHAPTER 12

LIGHTWORKER

IF WE ARE TO BELIEVE great things are happening, if we choose to see we are blessed, as opposed to seeing what's wrong with life, *then* we step into the flow.

The shift inside me had uncovered something deep, a new wisdom, a bigger awareness and a stronger faith. I now knew the spiritual path was limitless. I would always be growing and learning. Everything and everyone was teaching me in some way or another.

I'd never fully comprehended that I had this ability to shift so much, to find a new acceptance in the natural ebb and flow of life. I was free-flowing yet rooted to the ground. I felt like I was holding all the sacred magic of the world in my hands and I wanted everyone to feel it too. This was personal power that everyone could see and wanted a part of.

I saw the potential in all the people I met, in the heart of every child, every man, every woman and it excited me. I was like a magnet. Everywhere I went people wanted to be near me and would open up about their problems. Even strangers at a party or friends of friends would seek me out! I could channel divine messages. The angels would tell me who to call, who to text. I would have dreams about people and pass on the message they needed. I shared wisdom that helped them realise the 'specialness within themselves' that they were seeing in me.

"What you see in me is within you too," became my mantra.

I saw those I met awakening to something bigger. I shone a light so they could see their own path, discovering their own soul's purpose, just like I had. I helped people see again, believe again, even breathe again. They trusted me enough to take off their masks and I challenged them to clean up their negative belief systems, self-talk and heavy judgment towards themselves and others.

I taught forgiveness, compassion, letting go of unnecessary drama and toxic relationships by owning their responsibility rather than blaming everyone else or the way of the world. I loved nothing more than to see people step up into their personal power and find the freedom in their mind.

My mission was to help as many people as I could through meditation, mentoring, and Reiki. At times, I thought it was my 'one woman mission' to save the world, but I had to check my ego every now and then to remind myself I was not a saviour. People didn't need saving. I wasn't God.

I was here to be a messenger, a lightworker, to play a part in shifting the consciousness of the world, along with millions of others who were coming into bloom on the earth.

***

Paths apart

As we stepped into another new year, something wasn't quite right with Harry. The more confident and open I became, the more he pushed back. He'd roll his eyes at things I said or challenge me unnecessarily when I was high on life or sharing amazing miracles I'd seen happen.

He would tell me I'd changed, but I wouldn't see it. *I'm a better version of me! I'm happier. For fuck sake. What's his problem now?!*

Sometimes I would bite back, but most of the time I could make light of it. I'd turn it into a joke or turn up the music and dance in the kitchen to brush it off. Each time he belittled my beliefs, though, I shut down a little on the inside.

I didn't really want to share it with anyone, but every time I went to see my friend Sarah who would make my eyebrows look nice and generally tidy me up, I would cry and it would all come out.

"But Lou, you are different. You are constantly changing. You speak of things most of us don't understand. We love you, you know that, but sometimes you can seem a bit far out for all of us. Give him a little time, Lou."

I couldn't see it. I just thought I was me. But I trusted Sarah and I tried to hear what she was saying. *Maybe I am far out to people who don't feel the energy or believe in the Universe? Maybe I come across to some people like scientific academics come across to me. We're all different.*

We had a few gigs lined up, our version of 'date night.' Connecting over music was our thing and I loved the sense of wholeness we shared when we went out dancing. We headed back to our old stomping ground in London, Shepherd's Bush Empire. Harry was relaxed and happy, his arms wrapped around me as we watched the gig, when a woman walked through the crowd and passed out right at my feet. I crouched down below the crowd, held her and did Reiki on her until she got herself together again. She couldn't stop looking at me afterwards, thanking me.

"It was no bother, sweetie," I said picking her up.

Then she went on her way.

After the gig, I was chattering away as usual while Harry drove. I gushed at the amazingness of the Universe, the wonder and the miracles that happened every day, at how blessed I was to be so connected to the Reiki and do that for people. Harry's walls went up. He was cold with me and didn't want to talk.

"God, Lou, do we have to talk about this shit all the time?" he snapped.

I couldn't understand his reaction but stopped talking and looked out the window. I didn't want to feed the animosity, so I went to bed without saying anything. And there I began to close down too. I was fed up of his weird outbursts and now I was on lockdown. I felt nothing in my soul. I was just blank. I didn't even feel love. I was amazed I could even close my heart, but evidently I could. Then again, I had had a lifetime of practice when I was a kid. Closing down on someone saves you being hurt by them. I'd learned that one well.

When Harry went off to the office the next day, he didn't even say goodbye. Nothing like that had ever happened before and it frightened the hell out of me. Shaking, I texted him.

"What's happened to us, Harry? It's like a part of us has died. I'm so scared. I didn't even feel love for you last night. I'm sorry. I completely closed down on you. I felt nothing. It shook me. We need to sort this out. I love you x"

I got nothing back. I couldn't concentrate all morning. I tried calling. Nothing. Two hours later I got a message.

"Not ignoring you. Sending you an email."

After waiting for a lifetime, his email arrived.

Lou, a part of us hasn't died. It's just been lost. I agree it is broken and has been for a while. Saying that makes me scared to the point I feel sick. I will always give you everything I can. I will listen, offer advice where I can. Most importantly, I will learn to just accept who you are and where you are going.

Please don't stop telling me about what you are up to. Closing off would be the worst thing that could happen to us. I need you to accept that I might just not get it and it's okay for me to be like that.

Open your heart to me, Lou. You've taken yourself down a path that isn't mine. That's absolutely fine. You have every right to do that. I'm really not blaming you for anything, just trying to explain.

I know you've tried to include me and you would like nothing more than for me to take this journey with you, but the reality is I can't force myself to get to the same level as you. I'm not you. I've tried. I've really tried. But it's not me and it's not fair to expect me to change. This is your path, not mine, and that's cool.

You have to understand that you made the decision to go down this route and there was always a risk our paths would start heading in different directions. I suppose rather selfishly, truth be told, part of me just wants the old

Lou back, the one where we were inseparable, where we joked around and were on the same wavelength. It breaks my heart to think that's just a memory now, but it's something I need to deal with. And I promise you that I will. It sounds dramatic, I know, but I think it explains where we are at the moment. Heading in different directions. But I really do believe that we can turn this around.

There needs to be a much higher level of understanding from both of us in terms of accepting where the other is. I know I need to do this and I think that you do too. There is no reason why our paths can't head in the same direction. They always have up until recently and I'm certain they will again for the rest of our lives. We just both need to recognise that we're at a junction and have to make sure we take the same turning.

I know I'm probably difficult to be around at the moment. I apologise completely. I don't want to make excuses, but work, tax bills, Christmas, holiday, cars, generally anything that costs money are clearly having a bigger effect on me than I've been willing to accept. I could really do with some help here, but in all honestly, I don't feel I can talk to you about this. I'm afraid being told 'just trust the Universe' doesn't work for me at the moment. I've fucking tried, but I can't see much changing.

It's unfair for me to assume that you understand what I'm going through. How can you? You are not me. I need to learn that your way of dealing with things is different from mine. But I also need to learn from you how to deal with things. So please don't stop trying to teach me!

Lou, let's sort this out now. Let's bring our paths back into alignment and live our lives being awesome together.

*It's perfectly doable. We are not as lost as we think we are.
It just needs some understanding.*

I love you xx

***

The healer at the rave

By the next gig, the heaviness had lifted. We were playful again. We drank pints and giggled together.

Then a guy walked towards us through the crowd. He was alone, having a panic attack. I got hold of him before he lost it completely and sat on the floor of the crowded venue doing Reiki on him and bringing him round. He came good and we hugged before he went on his way. I turned around to find his friends busy telling Harry how grateful they were.

"Happens all the time, mate. Don't worry. It's like people know where to find her when they're in trouble," he said.

Internally, I was beaming. It was like Harry *got it!* Like he got me! Like he was not only accepting it, but proud of me too.

The third gig that week was an all-night rave in Brixton. It was our favourite venue in London at the old theatre with the slightly sloping floor. We had been coming to raves here since we were 20. Over the years, our age became more obvious, but we still loved it.

Dancing with our friends, I looked over and saw a kid about 18 years old. He was a few feet away, but I could see his energy field collapsing from where I stood. I felt his aloneness. He was so out of it. He looked like he was about to have a fit from taking too many drugs. I could see it a mile off.

I moved my way through the crowd towards him. He was shaking, vacant eyes. He looked terrified. I put my hands on his face.

"Darling, where are your friends?"

He was shaking too much to answer and I knew he was going to start fitting. I looked over to Harry and he met my eyes through the crowd. *Come here quick*, I mouthed. It was as if this kid knew he could let go. He fell to the ground, Harry catching him as he went.

We called security over and four of us carried him into the medical bay at the back of the club, unsympathetic lights glaring in his eyes. I could feel their coldness sending him further into the K-hole. There was no love, just medical people doing what they do with drug overdoses.

I sat by his head, pushed one hand under his back to reach his heart and put the other on top of his chest. I whispered in his ears, soothing him like a mother would, bringing his body back to stillness, his soul back to his body. His breath began to regulate. I breathed with him, showing him he wasn't alone and need not be frightened. I looked down towards his legs. There was Harry, both hands on this kid's feet, focusing deeply on channelling Reiki. I could see Harry's energy, like a guardian angel. *Oh my, you've stepped up*, I sent to him in my mind.

"If you don't know him, then you can leave," the medic said flatly.

With authority, Harry looked up at him and said, "We're not leaving, mate."

The medics left us to what we were doing, bemused but somehow knowing not to intervene. I felt parts of the kid begin to return to the world. And as the ambulance arrived to take him to hospital, I surrounded him with a golden light, and knew he would be fine.

Harry and I went back into the rave. We had done our work as a team and were both pretty pleased with ourselves!

***

Ego deaths

I heard the crash outside the house and knew it was my car. I ran downstairs and out the front door. And there it was, my BMW crumpled up with another car. I reached the road and found a young woman sitting in her car in shock. I helped her out, checking she was okay.

"Don't call the police, don't call the police," she begged. But the road was covered in glass; we had no choice.

"I need the toilet," she said through her tears. I comforted her and led her towards the house.

"Don't take her in there, Lou," Harry told me sternly, but it was too late.

I felt bad for her and wanted to protect her. I knew she would be arrested, she was so drunk.

"I fell out with my boyfriend," she cried.

Sorting out the car made me angry and upset. We got screwed over by the insurance company, which undervalued the car by thousands. I knew there was a lesson in everything, though, and when the reality hit that we had no car, I looked for the higher reason.

I recalled the intentions I had set at the start of the year. Stepping outside and looking up at the bright stars at 3am on New Year's Day, I'd whispered to the Universe, "I want to fully let go of my ego. I want to see my true self and not be dictated to by my ego's desires. I want to feel free from any unnecessary chains."

Oh, that's right! Now I could see it. The BMW was the last of my ego deaths. It became even more apparent when my father-in-law kindly and generously bought me a 14-year-old £500 run-around of a car previously owned by a neighbour's 17-year-old son. I was conflicted in gratitude for his sweetness yet my ego was screaming, *I cannot be seen driving this!*

And so I began the process of owning the ego death. When I wanted to park my old banger two roads away from the school, I made myself drive as close to the gates as possible and leave it in plain sight. When I wanted to hide my car from my students and clients, I was sure to make it visible. I put myself through the discomfort, so I could finally let go of that egoist chain. *This is your lesson, Lou. To learn not to care about what people think. To learn to own your 'success' even when the car you drive does not reflect that.*

And amazingly, within months, I truly didn't care! I was happy, even when a friend of mine laughed at me for driving it, even when people looked confused because everyone in our area drove posh cars and mine was quite a contrast. Then I realised they probably didn't think about it at all. I was just projecting my own shame. They had better things to think about than me and my car!

It was liberating in every way. I began to see how we humans are all trapped by what we think we *should* have, assuming people are judging us, and forgetting it's about who we are. And so what if they judge us? That says more about their insecurities than about us.

You can fly now

It was springtime and the builders had arrived to begin the house extension I'd been dreaming about for 12 years! That morning, I found a dead female blackbird on the doorstep. Our home was growing, as was I, as was Harry, so I didn't take it as a bad omen. Indeed, it was a death of the old. The next morning, there was a live blackbird on the doorstep, and there he stayed, from dawn until dusk, day after day after day.

Our lives were thriving in wonderful ways. We had shed layers of ego. We began to manifest good stuff again, but we were much more grounded about it. I realised when I stopped moaning about how shit the house was — the ice on the windows, the holes in the walls — and loved it for what it was, it would love us back. To manifest, we had to love what we had already.

As our house expanded, so did our souls. I began to release habits and people from my life that weighed me down. I stopped smoking. I was sick of it and didn't want to be in the cage any more. And that was the end of that. It was so easy in the end. I found a new part of myself that could commit and was determined to make better choices.

I was dedicated to a strong meditation practice and exercise routine. I was eating well. I had structure in my life. Because of all this, I was on fire, filling my Reiki classes, growing a huge community of students and selling out my mindfulness programs. I let go of the things that no longer served me, even when it was hard, even when sometimes I convinced myself I needed them in my life to appease my ego... like my breakfast radio show. I learned to say no and stopped trying to help *everyone*. I practised the art of the phrase, "Do you want to meet me for a coffee and a friendly chat, or do you need a session?"

I formed better boundaries. The clearer I was on those boundaries, the more it triggered people, but I had to look after myself and my time. I was getting messages every day from people telling me how their journey was going. My client base was building nicely.

And that little blackbird called all day long, day in, day out, trying to get my attention.

"Lou, turn the bloody thing off. Can't you talk to it or something?" the builders would joke.

By the time the summer came, we had grown used to meeting our blackbird every day. The sound of the drills and diggers drowned him out, but he tweeted on! Every morning after my meditation, I would sit and talk to that blackbird, while drinking my coffee and greeting the morning sun. He would come to me, worm in his beak, and still shout at me with his mouth full!

"Dude, I have no freaking idea what you want. You've got a worm. You're not hungry. But you want me to listen to you."

All day, all night. How the little thing kept on at us, I don't know, but he didn't stop.

One evening, we were on the sofa and the blackbird threw himself into the window. Another night, he flew backwards and forwards, shaving up close to the window. He had a message — I just knew he did — but I didn't understand what it was.

Finally, the TV turned on by itself and Paul McCartney was singing his famous lyrics about a blackbird taking its broken wings and learning to fly.

The blackbird brings an invitation to a sacred cosmic journey. Our blackbird was asking me to go with him. I had no idea where. And I didn't think life could get any bigger...

***

CHAPTER 13

THE SHAMAN

Soul agreements

FOLLOW THE GOLDEN threads of wonder and people will appear just when we need them, disappear when we don't, and some will stay a lifetime. It is thought that before we come to earth, we make agreements with the people who will come into our life to help us learn and grow. Each one will weave their thread into the tapestry of our life.

Some bring love and laugher. They may raise us so high that we grasp it, desperately hoping it will never end. Some bring lessons wrapped in pain, holding us in cages, paralysing us until we find an inner strength to move on. Some guide us through the darkness while we seek that something we never knew we had, growing us in ways we never knew we could. Some challenge our perspective, waking us up to new ideas, new pathways, new adventures. Some push us, dare us and awaken our passions, taking us to new lands, reaching new highs.

And then there are those special ones, the ones who are few and far between. If and when we are ready, they will appear in the most mysterious of ways. They are here to awaken the purpose of our soul.

This is the soul calling, the quests we take over and over again until we are prepared for the journey of a lifetime. Each time we complete these quests, consciously or unconsciously, we are preparing ourselves for the next level. Should you choose to ignore your call, you will find yourself trapped, stuck below a glass ceiling. You will become so numb that you forget to look up, because it is too painful to know there was something more. There is always something more.

To travel the greatest journey of your life, you must first learn to break through the glass ceilings that will keep appearing. You must learn to become one with the glass, to know it's as much a part of you as you are of it. This can only be achieved by facing your quests over and over and over again. There will always be rewards.

***

So, what exactly is a shaman?

I don't know what I was expecting, maybe a woman in a giant headdress and shamanic regalia, but this shaman was normal. More than normal — not even a joss stick or tie-dye in sight. She took a seat in the studio at the radio station, quietly, nervously. Doing radio shows made even the most confident people crumble, but I had a way of making them feel relaxed to the point of not wanting to shut up. Then, in came the medium, a beautiful lady from Sri Lanka, round face, large brown eyes, bubbly and excited.

When I'd offered to cover the mid-morning radio show for another presenter, I'd had no awareness that the two guests would be the catalyst for my highest soul purpose call. They were here to open the gateway to my destiny and they had no idea either.

For two hours, we chatted about all things crazy, spiritual and healing. We were giddy in each other's energy, digressing into the weird and wonderful of the spirit world. I'd never grasped what a shaman actually did and this woman talked about a medicine mesa that looked like a bag of rocks to me. She talked of the four elements, which spoke to me as a lover of Mother Earth, but I was still none the wiser as to what a shaman was exactly.

As we said goodbye, the medium gave me her number and the shaman left me a leaflet with an eagle on it. That leaflet sat on my kitchen worktop for weeks, moving from place to place like a lot of our junk and unopened letters that tended to pile up, whereas I was excited to book a session with Angela, the medium, and did that straight away. I was intrigued to see what sort of experience I could get from a session with her.

In Angela's living room, curtains closed, she had a message for me.

"There are a lot of guides around you and one is persistent. Your great-grandmother is shouting your name, as if to wake you up. She is asking about all these unopened letters, telling you to get organised, saying you're too laid back and need to get all these opened and filed away. You also need to think about updating your will. Get that done and then forget about it."

I felt sick. Only yesterday, I'd been thinking about doing it. Now fear flushed my body. *Shit, I'm going to die!*

"Your finances are a mess. You have no security. You will have some help, but you need to get more structure in your life," Angela said.

She was right. Harry and I were still flying by the seat of our pants every month. We'd learned to live without any real security. We always got by. Just!

"Ahhhh, you have a sense of success in you now. You and your husband are very close. He is a good man. You are together all the time. I see a big kitchen and family all around your table."

I felt a sense of relief. Indeed, we had dinner every night with my in-laws and the kids. I fed at least seven people every night around that table and I loved it that way.

"It is a cluttered kitchen. I see pens and artwork. There is joy all day."

This was a life I had created. Clients coming in and out of my home. Between clients, Harry and I would have coffee, lots of sex, fun and laughter together. It was the life I wanted. We didn't care that we didn't have the security of loads of money. We were so happy.

"Lou, you will be spending a lot of time away from your home and family, even moving away. I see you not there. You need to get some childcare. I see you will not be there much at all this coming year."

Fear rolled in. I felt a threat to my family.

"I don't think so," I scoffed. "We've finally got this life to where we want it. I won't be going away anywhere and certainly no-one else will be raising my kids other than me!"

"No, you're going away from your family. Something is taking you."

I went home and tidied the house. It needed doing anyway. Everywhere was chaotic. We never had a back-up plan for cash. We earned enough to get by and have a good time. Some months would be epic, some months not so epic, depending on what courses I was running. But money wasn't a major issue in our life any more. We seemed to be free of all that now. When Harry was down, I was up. And when Harry was up, I was down. Either way, one of us could bring in enough to survive.

For the next week, I kept seeing the leaflet floating around the house. It was for something called a medicine wheel, a four-week course spread over nine months, based on Peruvian Inca shamanic teachings. The way it was written, it was calling for people who were in bad times in their life, wounded people. I wasn't there. I'd done all that work. I was in a space where I could enjoy the rewards of having been in the cave. I shifted the leaflet from one side of the kitchen to the other for weeks, but never had gumption to bin it. It cluttered my new kitchen, calling to me every day to dial that number.

Eventually, I picked up the phone and spoke to someone. I don't even recall what the woman said to me. Whatever it was stoked a fire inside. She spoke of energy in a language familiar to me. Of Mother Earth and Grandfather Fire. Of coming back home to the earth. Of sacred medicine from the indigenous people. And I knew I had to go.

I could see it now though...

"Hey Harry, you don't mind holding the fort while I go off with a bunch of shamans into the woods for four weeks of this year, do you? Just have to go find myself some more. Oh, and I need £4000."

No way would Harry accept that.

I walked to the window, feeling the sun on my face, readying myself to tell this woman there was no way I could come on her course. I peered through the glass looking up at the sky... and a heron flew over. *Oh fuck, a heron! If that's not a nudge, then I don't know what is.*

"If the Universe wants me to come, I'll be there."

If I manifested the money, that would be sign enough for me that I was meant to go. Harry wouldn't be able to argue, because it would be clear it was out of our hands.

At dinner, I dropped into the conversation what I had spoken about to the woman. Harry didn't really take it in. I could feel that this was because I was manipulating the situation. I needed to be more authentic in getting myself to the course.

Something inside of me kept pointing me towards posting it on Facebook, sharing this situation. I shared everything else on social media. Why wouldn't I share this? But it didn't feel quite right and I kept pushing it away. Another weekend went by and I broached the subject with Harry.

"I want to do this course, but don't have the money. I'm sure if the money turns up, I will go," I said, hoping to tell him more than ask him.

On Monday morning, I awoke early to the same stirrings. *Post it on Facebook.* So I took out my phone and began to type, letting words just flow out my fingers:

I'll get by with a little help from my friends. I call upon you for your help! Okay, so this is a weird thing to post and so far out my comfort zone that my heart is fluttering! But I figure if it works, then it means I'm meant to do this. And if it doesn't, then that path was not for me. What I teach and how I heal has come from deep intuition and I have had some great teachers along the way to help me get where I am today — a Hindu yogi, Buddhist monk, my mentor Yoda and my Reiki Masters.

However, I am ready to go deeper. I want to learn more so I can bring it back to you lot, to speak, teach, heal and shine more love and light. But that means finding a new teacher — a shaman! I have a calling to go round a medicine wheel, a year-long course, but it starts in 10 days' time. Shit! If I miss it, I'll have to wait another year. NO! Life is too short to wait a year! The course means I can train to the next level of shamanic healing. WOW!

I want this, but every penny for the last year has gone into our house renovation. My pot is empty. So Universe, manifesting is needed! I need £850 in 10 days' time to do the first week. Can you help this money come to me? Maybe you want (or know someone who wants) to learn from me, heal, rise up and be fucking happy by doing my 8-week mentoring and Reiki course. That would be £815!

Within 23 minutes, I got a reply:

Lou, I've been wanting to learn from you for a while. Now I have some inheritance and I've been wondering where to invest it. Then I saw your post. I would love to train with you. And I can put it into your bank now.

This was a win-win. I was shocked, but I knew, I knew, I knew that this was meant to be. *Wow! Thank you, Universe. And all done in 23 minutes!*

"Harry, Harry, Harry," I ran around the house like an excited kid, "Guess what just happened! I knew if the Universe wanted me to go, I would manifest the money, and that's just what happened! Isn't it amazing?"

He was pissed off, really pissed off.

"That's not fucking manifesting, Lou. It's begging. You should be ashamed of yourself."

I refused to let this wobble me. I knew this had to happen. And I knew this was his pattern. He hated change. He resisted everything I did that involved me being pulled away. I knew I had to go though and I had to stand my ground until he came round.

"Baby," I said entwining my leg around his waist, "I understand that it feels like you're losing me to Jesus, God, the Universe, blah blah. And now I'm knocking around with a bunch of weird shamans shaking a rattle at a fire. But I need you to trust in us. Because something big is brewing. Know that no matter where I go, we may be apart for a few days, but we are always together. My life is nothing without you."

"I love you, you dickhead. Don't start wearing tie-dye or I'll divorce you," he said.

*****

The South in spring

I left on the Friday. I was emotional, excited, but more than anything, confident. I knew I was going where I needed to go, even though I had little idea what it was all about. As I drove down the M4 towards Wales, a heron flew over and I laughed out loud. A beautiful reminder that this was my path.

I entered the manor house deep in the middle of nowhere surrounded by trees, dumped my bags in my room and walked into a large room with a circle of about 30 chairs in the centre. I was the first there along with the guy who turned out to be one of the teachers. I watched as people from all walks of life entered the room one by one, young and old, men and women, some nervous like me, some confident — none fitting the stereotypical shaman look I'd had in my mind!

Today we would learn the South of the medicine wheel, which represented the path of the 'wounded healer' and the connection to Sachamama, the water serpent. We were there to shed our past selves, like Sachamama sheds her skin, letting go of what no longer served us, transforming old wounds and healing the heavy energy stuck within our light bodies, doing our own healing so we could heal others.

I poked fun at myself in my introduction.

"My name is Lou. I'm a healer and teacher. I'm well aware that my ego thinks I know everything there is to know, but I'm prepared to come with a beginner's mind and start again."

At times, I felt judged by the 'elders' of the group. I sensed I was being sized up, sussed out. There was a good dose of eye-rolling. *It's okay. I've got this. I'm not everyone's cup of tea.* Gracefully, I learned and honoured the teachings of the medicine wheel brushing off the collapse of my energy and the creeping insecurity that was entering.

The most important aspect was growing my mesa, a medicine bundle. These stones were going to hold the medicine of the Q'ero lineage of shamanism and my own medicine through my own healing. I loved the course, the ancient wisdom of the Q'ero and the way it was taught. I revelled in watching my teacher glow as her passion shone through. She was in her flow. I could even see similarities in how I taught my own students. Even though I found her captivating, I just couldn't shift the uncomfortable feeling that she didn't like me. *Are these just my issues coming up? Are they triggering that wounded child inside of me, the one who doesn't like not being liked? Or are they really being rude to me? Am I pushing their buttons too? They are human, after all. Everyone has issues.*

I did the work as best I could during my healing sessions with the other shamans, but this heaviness of not being liked and needing to be accepted by my teachers stuck around the whole week. In class, I watched myself become a shadow of the powerful teacher and healer I thought myself to be. I reverted into that innocent little girl who needed to be accepted. I began to turn down my light, played the fool with self-deprecating behaviour and just tried to be nice so I would be liked and accepted. It didn't work. In fact, it seemed to do the opposite.

Inside I knew I was playing out old stories of not belonging, not being liked, not being clever enough and waking up hidden hurts of the rejection I had experienced in this and many other lives. We were all here to go deeper into 'our stuff' so we could heal and transform into the medicine men and women we were here to be. *This is the work*, I reminded myself.

At night, my dreams were vivid. In those dreams, I would collapse and hide my powers away from the people of the past so they would like me and not hurt me. I saw ancient healers being burned at the stake for being powerful.

One evening, I wandered into the woodland on my own. I had found a favourite tree that I could stand inside. I played my favourite songs full whack through my headphones and danced in the tree. Both dancing and trees always made me feel better, more like 'me' again. It was there that my spirit guide spoke to me. *It's a gift learning to hold your power. You don't have to be liked. You are more powerful when you let this go.*

***

All the students and teachers stood around our first fire ceremony and I was pissed off. I had tried to engage in conversation with my teacher over dinner, only to find she was not interested in speaking with me, yet spoke to everyone else. I was being rejected and it hurt. I was done with feeling like I didn't belong, feeling pushed out. *I have walked a path and created a life where I don't have to be around people like this. I don't treat my students like that. Why is she treating me like this?*

I stared at the fire and began to speak with it in my mind. *If this is where I need to be, give me a sign.* I looked around the 30 faces shaking their rattles and watching the flames. Then the fire twisted, turned and blew a huge cloud of smoke right into my face. Every one of the faces looked at me. *This isn't my lineage*, I said to the fire in my mind. *I'm not coming back to the next course, I'm done with it.*

At that moment, my teacher raised her arms up over her head, commanding and powerful, and broke the silence.

"This is your lineage now," she said to everyone in circle.

It was unbelievable.

Fine, I thought indignantly. *I hear you, Grandfather Fire. I will stay on this medicine wheel.*

Walking back from the fire ceremony through the woodland, I noticed my rings were missing from my fingers. I had taken them off to do some healing during the day. Now my ruby, my opal, my engagement and wedding rings were all gone. I felt sick with fear. This could not be happening. I tried the healing room, interrupting the teachers in their meeting, but fearless anyway.

"I'm sorry. I need to check in here. I've lost my rings. These are my sacred rings. I need to get them back," I said frantically.

James, one of the teachers, looked at me calmly.

"Louise, you can do this your way, running around aimlessly, or you can do it my way and lie down here."

Quietly, I obeyed and sat on the floor next to him. He opened his mesa and I chose one of his medicine stones. We began.

As I blew my stories into the stone, I went back further and further in time. I cried when I saw myself as a little girl back on that holiday, telling the man I wanted to go home now. Then I had a powerful vision I had never seen before. I saw the earth below me. I was being made to leave my home. My *galactic* parents were making me go to the earth. *Oh my, I'm not even from here!* In the vision, I cried and cried, "I want to go home. I want to go home."

"Lie down, Lou," James instructed warmly.

I lay down. I blew the energy. I blew and blew, breathing heavily as I went deeper and deeper into another world, my home, where I was from.

"I want to go home," I screamed out loud, as I felt James pulling threads from me, threads of when I was with that man in that room. Threads of the pain I had felt when I had to leave the planet I was from. And then stillness came. I saw my real home. Not earth, but another planet, where everything was peaceful, bathed in golden waterfalls of light.

I was home.

***

I went up to my room and there were my rings, behind a little bottle of lavender oil. I laughed. It worked then, the healing. I sat on the bed telling Harry all about it over FaceTime. I knew it sounded completely mad, but I knew it to be true. Everything in my life made sense now.

He was laughing at me, "I always said you weren't from this planet."

"God, I miss you babe. I wish you were here to make love to me."

"You'll have to make love to yourself," he laughed.

It made me feel weird.

"I don't like doing that unless you're with me," I said coyly, "It feels like I'm cheating on you and you know me better than I know me. You're better at it than I am."

"Sounds like you need practice then," he flirted back.

It was like being given permission, but it triggered shame in me that I knew I needed to heal. Touching myself felt so alien, but I pushed through the shame and began to journey into a new spirit world, where I was flying like an eagle over corn fields. There was corn everywhere. I could feel the wind on my body. I was flying and flying. It was incredible. As I flew, orgasm flowed through me, gently, peacefully.

As I fell asleep into deep dreams of new lands, I thought how curious it was to see a corn field. Then I felt my spirit guide, a jaguar, lying next to me. She was with me now. And would be forever.

***

The next day in circle, we opened our mesas and were passed a dried ear of corn.

"What's this?" I asked, amazed.

"In Peru, corn represents abundance. We feed our mesas with corn and flowers so our mesas are nurtured too. Then we are nurtured. Our mesas are a part of us and we are a part of them."

"Corn was in my vision last night," I said, giggling on the inside but trying to keep a straight face.

I had a revelation in that moment. Not only was I being gifted a lineage that I was connected to many lifetimes ago, but I was also healing around abundance. I knew if I kept releasing, sexually, emotionally and physically, I would be lighter and more able to receive abundance to help me walk the path.

I was a natural shamanic healer. I had done big work this week. I was confident with the medicine. I could track the creation stories to big wounds, going deeper and deeper into the stories of the other shamans to help them clear and transform. I could see how their energy shifted and changed, freedom from past pains igniting a new fire. I held three new medicine stones in an old embroidered cloth from my great-great-grandmother. That was my mesa now and it was growing to be part of who I was, who I'd always been.

I went to say goodbye and thank you to the main course teacher, but she turned her back on me. I left without saying a word. I couldn't believe I was putting myself through this rejection and judgment, but I knew this was where I needed to be.

On the way home, the trees held me and the angels played songs on the radio just for me. As I wondered if I would return to the medicine wheel, a heron flew over again. I squealed with delight, *My beautiful spirit guide. Thank you for coming.* I felt her reply, *Well done, Louise. You're on the right path. Thank you for showing up.*

At home, we lay on the bed — two girls, two cats, me and Harry, all chatting. He was gazing into my eyes as I told them about my week.

My connection to the four elements felt deeper than before, Mother Earth, the waters, the air... certainly, I had a deeper relationship with Grandfather Fire. I felt them all stronger now than I had in my life. We communicated much more deeply. And I knew now how to connect with the energies of my serpent, jaguar, hummingbird and eagle.

The ancient Q'ero medicine and Mother Earth, Pachamama, were so close I could touch them.

***

The West in summer

I assumed it would land in my lap, like the last lot of £850, because that's what the Universe does, doesn't it? But nothing came. More than ever, we were broke after a tough month. I lay at the top of the garden crying. I had 12 hours to raise the funds. *Why is the Universe being such a tight-arse fuck? It knows I have to go. It wants me there. Why hasn't the money come? I was cross and confused, and a sense of failure was heavy within me.*

I lay with my head pointing towards a cherry blossom tree. I talked to the trees whenever I felt lost or confused. There would always be a message if I was quiet enough. Something told me to turn my head, and as I did, a heron swooped before my eyes. *Holy shit!* I had never seen one fly so close, and not for months, since coming home from the

South earlier in the year. The message was loud and clear. *One way or another, I'm going to be there.*

I rang my teacher to tell her my predicament. She was matter of fact.

"This is classic behaviour of the energy you're stepping into. Raise the money for the accommodation by tomorrow. Pay me the rest by the end of the summer."

I came back down the garden, wiping my tears. *The good news is the heron came and now I only need £350 for tomorrow*, I thought. *The bad news is still no money has come in.* £350 was all I had, including for the mortgage.

"Just take it. I'll figure something out," said Harry. "Just go and pack your bags, babe."

What was going on? Where was his classic resistance? Where was the man who never wanted me to go?

As I left for Wales, I saw my sign that everything would be alright: another heron. *Bloody hell, Universe, you can send me herons. Can't you send me the £850?* The clock turned 11:11 as I thought it — another cheeky wink.

It was a week of learning the way of the peaceful warrior, the rainbow warrior, and going into the work of Carl Jung, the famous psychotherapist. I knew the theory — that there was so much about ourselves we could not see, parts of ourselves we deny — but I had never really had the space to explore this within myself. It was powerful. *We think people can't see this in us, but they can*, I realised. *I am pointing my finger at my teachers saying they are rejecting me, but where am I rejecting myself?* We were our own sorcerers, after all. We were the ones who create these situations. We were the ones who made ourselves available to being treated in a certain way. It was our job to go to the root of issues and heal them, so they didn't drive current behaviours any longer.

We also studied Karpman's famous concept of the drama triangle. My mum was a Relate counsellor, so I was aware of Karpman's drama triangle, but again I had never explored how I participated in it. I had always been able to project drama onto other people. Now it was my own chance to see. I faced my own shadows and there it was. I was being a victim, playing my own drama, manifesting a perpetrator in my teachers.

***

Sent from the stars

"You're an indigo child," Wendy said to me as we walked back from the fire ceremony one evening. She was one of the wisest people I knew, like she had already devoured every book in the world.

"You're from the Pleiades. That's what your vision was about."

"What's the Pleiades?" I asked.

"The Seven Sisters star system, just up from Orion's Belt."

I looked at her dumbfounded.

"I've been obsessed with that star system all my life. I would feel pain when I couldn't see it in the sky."

"Of course you would, my darling star child. The ancient Q'ero believe we were sent from the stars to bring the world back into being, to play our part in the evolution of consciousness. You've been trying to hide your indigo light.

You think we can't all see your power, but we can!" she laughed.

"How do you know all that? You're so clever. I wish I knew this stuff," I said, hugging her.

"Don't project 'you're so clever' onto me, Louise Carron Harris. What you see in me is what is within you," she reminded me.

On my drive home, I felt a deep sense of gratitude and began talking to the Universe. *Am I really a star child? Is that why I saw the stars the night Avalon was conceived? Are my girls star children too? Is this cosmology true? Is that where I'm from? Give me a sign...*

And there she was, my heron. And I knew.

***

The storytelling call

My old friend Emma randomly messaged me and asked if I wanted to take the kids to watch a storytelling show in London called *I Believe In Unicorns*. She knew me. I was unicorn-obsessed!

I needed to break away from the monotony of home where we had spent the whole of the summer holidays. We were tight financially *again* and had no money to go on holiday. Part of me was going to say no even to a London day trip because of finances, but another part said *just go*.

We gathered into a dreamy little theatre, and I sat in awe, captivated by one woman on stage. She drew me into her most magical story. Bells went off in my head. I wept. She was showing me what I was being called to do: to be on stage to tell stories like she was doing! But how did this fit with my work?

I wanted to find out, so I followed the threads... by stalking her on Twitter!

"Please teach me how to do what you do," I messaged her.

"Send me your number and I'll call you."

I couldn't believe she even replied, let alone offered to speak with me. When the phone rang, I was blown away by her generosity.

"It sounds like I have some guidance you may need. I sense we are meant to meet. Let's do coffee," she suggested.

I was all in.

***

In awe of this incredible woman, I sipped my coffee and watched the way she spoke. She knew me, even though she didn't know me. I was sure she was an earth angel.

"You have all these roles in your life, Louise. I sense that you're going to pull them all together. Before it reveals itself to you, you need to go on a storytelling course. It's a four-week program starting next year. My teacher Sue is the facilitator. You'll soon see how all these threads come together to make the bigger picture of your life. Just be patient while it unfolds."

Harry backed my decision to do yet more training the following year, which left me amazed. *Not an ounce of push-back from him... how weird!*

I had another thread to follow.

And another course to go on... unaware that I would soon have a story of my own to tell.

Going sober

The awakening comes when you know you have to follow your heart even though the rest of the world says you're mad. They do their best to keep you where you are, because it means their world doesn't have to change. They don't want you to change, because they are not ready. But you are safe to take the steps if you stay still in your mind, your body, your spirit. Your people will support you in the end.

This summer was hard for me. The medicine wheel was changing me again, and I was struggling, because everyone else was conflicted by my changes. Once again, it caused tensions between Harry and me. I changed. He resisted. I was fed up of him always pulling me back and needing me to be who he once knew me to be: Party Lou.

The breakthrough came when we went away to a beautiful manor house in Dartmoor for Karina's 40th birthday. It was dark when we arrived on the Friday night at 22:22. Forty of our friends had gathered to celebrate this awesome occasion, but I was exhausted and went straight to bed leaving everyone else drinking and catching up. I woke early to see the most incredible woodland through my window. Excited, I jumped out of bed in my pyjamas, chucked on my trainers, grabbed my mesa and headed out to the trees.

It was magical. Ancient, old and rich. I looked around me in awe, tears rolling down my face. Wow! I had not known this was here. I went deeper into the woods and found a spot to stop. Time began to slow. Faces appeared from the trees. *Oh my!* They came alive, the tree people, tree goddesses, showing themselves to me.

Opening my mesa, I shared with them my fears. I tracked into the unease in my body. Tonight, there would be a big party; I was expected to be the life and soul, the last one standing, the tornado of wild energy in the room... and I didn't want to do it.

I wanted to stop poisoning my body with alcohol. I was done with getting 'out of it', over feeling ill for two days after every 'session', fed up of the eczema on my face that flared up every time I drank making it red and raw all over. I felt unattractive, unhealthy, ugly even, yet I was gripped with emptiness. If I didn't drink, what would I do? How would I be? How would I connect with everyone?

I meditated and journaled in the healing womb of the woodland for over an hour, hearing the river waters far in the distance. I was part of this magical place, my roots in the earth. I dreamed of a new world, a world where all colours and creeds connected, where we all felt safe on the belly of our Mother Earth, where we felt no separation, where we didn't need to seek beyond ourselves, where we all knew: it's all right here inside.

By the time I came back to the house, everyone was getting up for breakfast, nursing their hangovers and lounging around in their pyjamas.

That afternoon, I wandered the grand English manor house wondering how I was going to navigate the evening to come. Everyone had already started drinking in the late afternoon sun. Music was playing and life took on a sepia tone. I wanted to jump right in with a beer, but something was saying no. Not knowing what to do with myself, I took myself back to the woodland.

The tree goddesses looked strong and powerful, whispering to me on the winds, speaking to me through my heart. They were helping me work through the fear of separation in my mind, the loss that was happening as I began to accept that I needed to remain sober. *Help me stay sober tonight. I want to feel beautiful, powerful, goddess-like. Hold me. Help me make decisions that are right for me. Share your goddess energy with me. Guide me in making the right choices.* I felt the trees holding me. Something shifted. Already I was stronger. I felt a oneness with the tree goddesses. Grateful for their support, I walked confidently back to the house.

When I walked back through the door, my friends' dog Penny began to bark at me. She was going crazy, as if she'd forgotten who I was.

"I'm so sorry, Lou. I don't know what's gotten into her. She never does this," they said, grabbing the dog.

I knew why Penny was barking at me: my energy had altered and I carried the mystic energy from the woodland. I went to my room, found my sparkly dress, and did my hair and make-up. Already my skin glowed. *This is working!* I looked different, beautiful, a far cry from a few hours earlier. And yes, I felt powerful and goddess-like.

Harry was impressed with his wife and we walked down the grand stairs together. My friend Pete took one look at me.

"Wow, Lou! You look hot! What's happened to your skin? It's cleared up. You look amazing!"

He was always the first friend to tell me when I looked shit, my lack of fashion sense meaning he always commented on the way I looked. If Pete said I looked hot, that was confirmation of an outward change. And a definite win.

I decided not to tell myself I couldn't drink, but to tell myself I would make the best decision at the time. My girlfriends handed me a gin and tonic, a ritual we had had for years, pre-party drinks and a natter. I sipped it with them, chatted and laughed, enjoying their energy and loving them with such gratitude for being in my life. I had no intention of drinking the gin; only a few sips to not draw attention. I realised that I had shifted my consciousness so much that I didn't even want it. I held that glass with me all night and no-one was any the wiser, though I always had a cup of peppermint tea nearby.

I DJed, danced like a goddess and partied like Party Lou even though I was sober. At 3am, I went to bed, not because I wanted to, not because everyone else was drunk, but because my hips hurt so much from dancing. Normally, I'd have been too far gone to notice. Harry partied on without me and it was strange to go to bed without him, but I was so proud of myself that it didn't matter. I wanted him to have a good time.

Two hours later, I woke to Harry standing at the foot of the bed, fully dressed in army gear from the 1920s, an air rifle included.

"We found the secret gun room," he slurred with a smile.

I burst out laughing and couldn't stop, "Fuck off, you weirdo, and go put that bloody gun away!"

I was glad he was happy, strange as it was that I wasn't on the adventure with him. There was peace inside me as I drifted back to sleep. A few hours later, feeling fresh and smug, I woke next to Harry, who was snoring away, booze sweating from every pore. He was going to feel like hell in a few hours. I kissed him on his forehead and headed down to the woodland to give thanks to the tree goddesses for holding space for me while I evolved.

***

CHAPTER 14

THE END IS JUST THE BEGINNING

Could this be it?

I BEGAN TO TELL him about a new vision I'd had, where I was leading a fleet of boats, sailing through a sea of consciousness, and how I had been getting more visions of Jesus, but he seemed annoyed at me talking away. His energy was defensive. Harry rarely spoke, but I could read every part of his energy field as well as his body. That word "Jesus" triggered him, but it wasn't just the Jesus thing.

Again, everything had changed in the last month since the summer had begun to draw to an end. Autumn seemed to wake my instinctive need to shed. As had been the case for many years, the last few months of the year saw me shifting and Harry felt pushed into making these changes too. But he didn't want to go there. Not again. I wanted to close the offices and work from home. We didn't need them. They were just for ego and they cost us a lot of money. I'd also gone and gotten myself a new tattoo without him, which he suggested took away from the sacredness of our matching infinity tattoos from the previous summer. Plus, I'd become friends with the local vicar and loved chatting to him which made him fear I was going to run off and join the church.

Individually, any of these would have been enough to undermine our sense of stability. Yet the real issue for Harry was something else entirely. I'd gone sober.

Instead of perching ourselves at the breakfast bar on a Friday night, drinking and chatting together, he went and watched TV, and I went into the garden to make fires and play with my mesa. Our sacred Harry and Lou nights in had vanished. Distance had come in and we didn't know how to get back to each other. We hadn't found a way to integrate the changes and Harry was starting to push back. We had been here before, but what had kept us together was getting shit-faced and having lots of sex.

Over a period of a few weeks, it got incredibly hard between us. We had never really argued for more than 24 hours, but the residue of constant change brought a heaviness into our house that none of us were used to. The more I felt judged by him, the more I closed down. The more I withheld from him, the further into myself I went. I was going deeper into my world, the world that was full of wonder to me. Then I would find him trying, trying to bring me back to him, but unless our hearts were fully connected, I couldn't open to him in mind nor body. I didn't want to give him any part of me if he couldn't accept me for me.

And he was shutting down on me, too. I woke up one morning and felt like he hated me. I didn't recognise him. It was frightening. *God, is this what happens to people when they divorce?* If he stayed like this forever, he would forget who I was and I would forget who he was. Could we end up apart from each other, hating each other? The realisation of how fragile we were rocked me to the core.

We began to argue about all sorts of shit that wasn't really the problem. Then one Saturday morning, it blew up. My fury, my fear, my sadness, my blame all came out. Before I knew it, my phone was flying full pelt at the wall. I thought I'd smashed it to smithereens, because the force had been brutal, but I didn't hang around to find out.

I grabbed my keys and got in the car. I wanted to put my foot down and drive 100 miles an hour, but I heard my guide, *Slow down. Other people's lives are more important than your rage.* A scream fell from my mouth and surprised me. It carried on and on. When it came to an end, I screamed again. The energy, the anger flew out of my body. Part of me was embarrassed at my behaviour, but the shaman part could see this was a much-needed release. And through chaos came clarity.

I was so fucking fed up of everything, caught between my love for Harry and my need to honour my soul's purpose on this earth. I went to the only place that accepted me. The river. I fell to my knees and sobbed like a baby. Everything was falling apart around me again. Would this cycle never end? Would it always be like this? I had lost all control. I was so angry with him, with myself, with God.

Deep down, I knew I was crying because I felt so many parts of my ego — life as I knew it — falling away from me. I was no longer queen bee at the radio station. I no longer had a business that was going to make me millions and buy me a house with a pool. I no longer had an office with a nice postcode. I was no longer cool or funny or even sexy. I was not who everyone wanted me to be anymore. I wasn't who I wanted to be anymore.

Here suddenly, I wanted to be cool again. I wanted to be the popular girl who stripped down to her sexy underwear and played in the fountains at after-parties, because then I wouldn't be feeling like this. It would be easier to be that, to want that, but I was a sober fucking shaman, who talked to trees and Jesus. I didn't have any choice. I would never be that girl again. She was gone. And we all had to accept it.

Red-faced, I reached my favourite bench. The sun was warm and I watched a family playing with fishing nets. *That should be us, out enjoying the day.* Pain travelled through me at the thought of missing out. I kneeled down and sobbed into the ground, Pachamama, Mother Earth. *Hold me, Mama. I don't understand what is going on. Please hold me through this and help me see what I can't see.*

Harry not accepting the shift was a reflection of my inner world. I knew that. How could anyone love and accept me for me, if I didn't love and accept myself? But maybe this time loving myself wasn't going to be enough to bring him along. Maybe this was the point when Harry would wash his hands of me and all my weird stuff, and go back to the normal world. Maybe this was where we parted. Maybe I needed to wander this path alone.

I picked myself up from the ground and headed home. I had fucked my phone. I had fucked everything. I had lowered myself to that outburst, lost control, created a major fucking drama. There was nothing in me. I was exhausted, defeated, done.

I walked into the kitchen and he wouldn't look at me. He was furious still and I became furious within. Everything locked down inside. I felt the rage and hatred build. I blamed him, I realised. He started this.

"We need to talk," I said.

He was cold, disgusted with me, hanging on to the fact I had smashed my phone.

"Well, your phone is completely fucked."

"I don't care about my phone," I said under my breath.

"Well, maybe you should care."

"I don't fucking care about the fucking phone, Harry! I care about the fact that I think our marriage is more broken than the fucking phone and the phone is fucked beyond repair. This is about me changing. This is about me becoming something you don't want me to become. This is about us not being able to make it. This is about us falling apart, and the Harry and Lou show closing down. This is the beginning of the end for us. Neither of us can deny it anymore. This is where the fucking story ends."

I was shaking. I was screaming. And I saw his eyes change from anger to fear. He was as surprised at what was coming out of my mouth as I was, but I was numb and couldn't feel the words. It was like someone else was shouting through me. I had left my body. I closed down emotionally and continued.

"I'm not that girl anymore, Harry. She has gone. You either have to accept that or move on. And I don't blame you for wanting a normal wife and a normal life. But I can't be a part of this shit any more. I don't want to get drunk and fucked up anymore. That's not who I am. It's who I became just to be safe and accepted in the world. That's ego. Who I am underneath those behaviours is still me. I've changed, yes, but my essence is still the same. We change and grow. That's what we do when we grow up and grow old together.

We're not going to be the same 'you and me' that we were 17 years ago and we won't be the same 'you and me' in 17 years' time. And if we were, that means we got stuck somewhere along the line and stopped growing and exploring life. If you need someone who is normal, I understand, but I won't be normal for you or anyone because I would be doing myself and my life a disservice. I would be doing our kids a disservice because I want them to grow up exactly as they are, not trying to be who they think they should be!"

He was nervous. If I had known what I was truly saying, I would have been nervous too. Instead I was raging, talking without thinking.

"Come on, Lou. Let's go and sit in the Room of Requirement and talk."

We sat in silence, him trying to make it all okay.

"Lou, we can work this out."

"No, we can't!" I snapped.

I had the power, the ammunition to hurt him because I shut him down. I had never been so removed from Harry. I didn't know myself. I didn't know him. The words leaving my mouth came from somewhere beyond me.

"We need to separate. This isn't going to work anymore. We need some space."

We both stared at the wall for what felt like a lifetime. I was cut off. I couldn't even feel his energy. More words began to fall from my mouth, breaking the silence.

"I'll move out. It's not fair the other way. I'll have to go to Mum's for a week or two to figure out what I'm going to do, but I won't move the kids from their family home. I can take them with me this weekend if you need some space, or I can leave them if you would rather. We'll just have to make sure we are doing the best for them at all times."

I had never said such things in our 17 years together. I was cold, clinical, unbelieving of the words, like it wasn't me speaking. He didn't move. We fell back into silence. I followed the irregular nicks in the wallpaper with my eyes, recalling how Mum and I had decorated it only a month before. It was nice in here finally. Grown-up.

"I won't take the kids. This is their home. This is your home. But I will find somewhere to live, a shared room maybe or a studio flat. I'll get a job and we'll juggle the kids the best we can, but in the meantime I'll go away for a few days, just to get my head together. I'll look at jobs and places to live, then I'll come back down here. Please just give me a week to get my shit together."

This was the only way. There was no emotion behind it. I was detached from the consequences, detached from my life as it was. In the moment, this seemed the best decision.

"We don't need to do this, Lou. We don't."

"Yes we fucking do, Harry. Yes we do. If you ask me to choose between my calling and you, I *have* to choose my calling."

His head dropped. His face was blank. His energy was no longer desperate or fearful. Just sad.

"I always knew I was second in line. I always have been."

And in that moment, I woke up. I felt him. And I felt awful for how much he was hurting. I understood how I had been — always off somewhere leading, pleading, charming the world, letting everyone into our life. And he'd never said anything. He'd just gone along with it. The more I grew into my personal power, the further I flew away from him, the more he clung to me, desperate to keep me close to him. The only way he could have me, the only time I would disconnect from being in constant service to people and the Universe was getting drunk together, having sex and falling asleep when the sun came up.

The air was thick with the prospect of what we had to do. Like droplets of acid rain, it dripped into place in my mind. I couldn't feel the truth of what the words would mean, not being Harry's wife, not being a full-time mum, not living in this house that had been home for 13 years, not being part of this family, not having this name. My mind was black and white. Any droplets that touched me stung. My soul running from the pain, I recoiled back to the numbness. I knew the words had come from somewhere. I knew I had no idea what was happening, but something was about to change dramatically.

As I began to dismantle our life in my head, I looked at the pile of journals, books, vision boards, diaries and jars that I pulled out every full moon and new moon containing all my wishes, words, notes, feathers, trinkets, crystals. I had spent the last 10 years dedicated to my spirituality, the Law of Attraction, personal development, writing every day, planning, playing with the Universe. I had dedicated the last five years to my soul's calling to find my purpose here on the earth, to healing myself, to becoming better.

This house seemed to have chosen us all those years ago. This tiny room was a room of change, where I did my healing work. So many people's lives had changed in this room. In the time we had lived here, this room was the heart of our home. This room had transformed as we had. Once filled with 20-somethings playing at being adults, using mismatched crockery and chipped wine glasses, it had evolved into a party room, drapes of neon-painted sheets hung from the wall, a UV light in the corner, friends dressed in togas tripping on the floor in a haze of smoke. Then I painted it red. The demi-grand piano from my childhood was delivered and it took over two-thirds of the room. We set up some turntables on top, a pair of waist-high speakers in the corner, disco lights with bar stools around it!

When I was pregnant, we managed to squeeze a desk in against the back wall and it became the first office of my first business. Four years later, Harry had quit his job and needed a space. I wept when we sold the piano but rejoiced when Harry built two desks into the alcoves, side by side. We would sit day and night growing our business together, big dreams to take over the world. At night, the office became a party room, sometimes just the two of us, sometimes 22 of us, dancing until 5am, jumping off the desks and crowd-surfing as the kids slept upstairs. It was beautiful mayhem, a space of safety for many of my introverted friends, who found liberation in freely dancing in a home without judgment. Reaching new highs in these four walls was the glue of our long-lasting friendships rooted in the sacred ritual of dance and deep humility.

The Room of Requirement was a black hole of wonder. It was too hard to let go of the party, too hard to imagine a life with no booze, no dance, no playfulness. *This is who I am. I take people on a journey up to the stars. And this room is the shuttle.*

When Harry had unscrewed the desks from the walls to make it the grown-up room we were sitting in right now, I'd cried. I didn't want to grow up! We'd had sex in every corner of this room. I'd fallen pregnant over that desk. That desk had seen too many people dancing on it. These walls held every secret of every client and was home to my spirit guides.

We sat in silence for what felt like an eternity, both staring ahead. I couldn't bear to feel into his energy. I didn't want to leave and I didn't want to stay. Then his arm reached across his chair and he opened his hand in front of me. And I reached my arm over to him and put my hand in his. We sat holding hands, eyes still locked on the wall.

"Lou, this is not what I want. Is this what you want?"

"No, of course it's not what I want, babe," I admitted, emotions pouring from my eyes at last and my diaphragm gripping in devastation. An enormous sob came like a wave of relief through my body.

"I want to be with you, Lou," he had tears in his eyes too, and his face was pained and pale. I had never in all our years seen this look. He was broken and serious, but he was taking back control.

"Lou, I've never wanted anyone but you. I don't want us to split up. The idea is crazy to me. I want us all to be together. We have to find a way to make this happen. We have come this far. We can make our way through this. We can make it to the end. What do you think?"

I wanted to say yes. But I couldn't promise him that I could be who he wanted me to be. It was unfair to ask him to come with me on my journey or to understand what I didn't understand myself. It was unfair of me to put all this on him, but I couldn't live on this earth and not be who I was meant to be, who I was capable of being. And that seemed to make him unhappy. I said all this. He urged me to reconsider.

"We'll make it work like we've made everything work, Lou. We've been through so much. I know things have to change and I'm trying — I really am — to honour your shamanic journey. I think I do well at it most of the time. It's just that you fly so far away sometimes and I just don't have a chance to catch up. I want to support you; I need you to support me too. I'm sorry I've found it hard, but I think we need a new way to connect. I'm having to grieve a little at the loss of what we had before. That's not to say the future won't be as awesome. We just have to find the new way."

"I love you. You know that. I think you're the most amazing man in the whole Universe. Everyone does. And you are, apart from when you're being a cunt, but that's normally because I'm being a cunt too. But listen. I need you to understand, babe, my soul is calling for something. I can't describe it, but it feels like all this recent change is leading to something. I don't know where or what, but I can't jump back on the party train, and I need your support in that."

He took a breath.

"We need a replacement for all the parties and late nights. Can we start there? Looking for something new to do together? Maybe you could come and light some shamanic fires with me."

"Maybe you could come and watch shit TV and football with me," he laughed.

"Okay."

"Okay."

And just like that the world of Harry and Lou was restored. We came back to our centre point. The world felt safe again. As if all of that drama was from another lifetime.

***

Starting again

"Wanna come on Mary's vision board workshop with me, babe?"

"Sure."

"*Erm*, did you just say yes?"

"Yes, I said yes."

"Okay, I'll pay and I'll go, but please don't feel like you need to come because of me. You have to go because you want to."

"Yes, Lou, I'll come."

"Okay, so it's not cheap, just so you know. I'll pay for both of us to go. Say now or forever hold your peace."

"Yes, Lou, I'll come with you!"

I was so surprised. He was normally too self-conscious to do anything like that. I booked and was excited. This was going to be awesome. I loved being involved in the growth of Harry's business, helping him get focused and on fire. And I knew how powerful Mary's vision board workshops were.

On the morning of the workshop, he pulled out.

"I can't go. I've got too much work on."

Outwardly, I was mad with him.

"If you're committed to something, you make the time. But I see you manifested extra work so that you could get out of doing our class, because you never really wanted to go in the first place."

But deep down, I was more gutted than mad. I wanted him to share my vision. I wanted us to plan our next steps together.

I rocked up late to the vision board group. No-one there had ever seen me mad before. They hadn't witnessed what had been going on these past few months. I sat down to make my vision board. I cut and pasted and cut and pasted.

After three hours, I looked at it and what I saw scared the shit out of me. *What the hell have I created? Where are all the angels? It felt serious.*

All my past vision boards had couples on them, children, nature... This one was radically different. In the centre was a naked woman on the phone looking like no-one would ever mess with her. Next to her was a woman marching *on her own*. There was a picture of Australia, mountains, the Amazon jungle.

I wasn't aware why I had put any of these pictures on there. I'd just grabbed and stuck and grabbed and stuck. It frightened me.

Yet, there was magic in this board even if I wasn't quite ready to see it.

***

I wasn't surprised any more when I saw number sequences, but I was being shown something new. Everywhere, every day, I was seeing 999 and I knew that was the call-to-service number. I was waiting for whatever this call was.

"Lou, I heard that you're unhappy with your board. Seeing as Harry didn't do his session, how about I come over and do a reading of your board instead?"

I breathed a sigh of relief at Mary's suggestion. Only the day before, my shaman brother Simon helped me work through a little of what it meant.

"Sounds like Shaman Lou is stepping up and Fluffy White Clouds Lou is no more. You have to own your medicine woman."

Mary and I sat in the Room of Requirement drinking tea, staring at my vision board.

"Lou, tell me what you see. What colours do you have?"

"Mainly oranges and greens."

"What's this image?" she asked, pointing at a sea vista from a clifftop.

"Travel with the kids."

"What's this image about?" she indicated the huge map of Australia.

"I suppose it's to represent Sandy, my best friend. I would love to see her. She lives there now. I miss her so much my heart hurts. I just don't have the £10,000 we need to get us all over there for a holiday."

"Mmm, this feels big, like you need to go there."

The doorbell rang and I jumped up to answer it. On the doorstep was a bunch of flowers left by the delivery man. I sat next to Mary, fiddling with the tag to see who they were from. The message read:

No reason, just because I love you, love Sandy xxx

"Well, if that's not a sign to say you need to get to Australia, I don't know what is."

We laughed and I let go of having to understand the rest of the vision board.

"I'm going to make this happen."

"I'm sure you will!"

***

Decluttering the old to bring in the new

I began decluttering after that session, clearing space to manifest something, though it was already happening naturally. I let go of my new music radio show, which meant giving up radio all together. It was time to let the younger ones have the opportunity. I sorted out my house, cleaning, clearing, tidying up old emails, throwing away clothes I didn't wear. Then I went into a healing state and did some emotional decluttering of my soul.

I was also unearthing old pains, deep wounds. Some days bring up all your stuff — everything. All the shards of glass, hidden away, come back to say, "I'm still here. I may be silent, I may be hidden in the domains of your soul, but I'm still here waiting to be healed." When you agree that it's time to face that part, to open that can, acknowledging you are ready, the Universe makes sure everything is in line for you to heal.

So that's what happened. A random friend arrived for a chat, offered to take the kids. Harry brought his healing hands to my heart as I fell asleep sobbing into the depths of my old, old pain. I drifted in and out of the dark place and swam through murky waters alone. All alone. Just my spirit, no ego.

And I recognised my spirit, even all alone. *I am so strong, so powerful, so beautiful, so blessed.* As I swam through the darkness, I had no fear. Everything was as it was meant to be.

With every wound I healed, I transcended higher. With every wound we will heal, we all will transcend higher.

***

We were letting go of the offices, handing back the keys after five years. Harry came in with the last of our bits. Nostalgically, I looked over the leaflets of my old company.

"I always thought I would sell it to someone who loved it as much as me."

At that moment, it clicked. I remembered an old client saying she loved my company so much she wanted to buy the brand, the contacts and the website for £10,000. That was two years ago, but I messaged her anyway.

Random thought, but do you still want my old company?

She texted back.

I was just walking the dogs and thinking of you. I wanted to ask you about it. The answer is yes!

I was utterly shocked but buzzing. Harry was not.

"Babe, it means we can go away and do what my vision board has been calling me to do!"

"Lou, I have a tax bill that needs to be paid."

"Fuck the tax. This money is for Australia. We have to go. This is the Universe calling. Plus, something keeps telling me we need to go to that giant rock thing. I think it's called Uluru. We need to go there!"

I made plans with Sandy anyway.

"We'll be there in March," I told her.

That was only five months away and felt like no time compared to the three years she had been gone.

It took Harry a few days to see my mind was set. I was so grateful for him. He had met me where I was and allowed me to push him to places he didn't want to go. My beautiful soulmate, he had already watched me being pulled so many places that he could not enter and was still here next to me, stepping outside his comfort levels.

And now, with a little money, we had breathing space.

***

The North in Autumn

At the next training, I told all my fellow shamans about the magic that had happened.

"I can't believe I've manifested on such a huge scale. It's a miracle!"

Everyone was excited for me and wanted to learn how I'd done it.

Aptly, this part of the medicine wheel was teaching the way of the hummingbird, learning to hear the call, answering it, and saying yes! It was about manifesting the world we wanted.

I felt like a manifesting queen already and thought I had stepped into this part of the wheel. I wanted everyone else to step into it too. I was excited for me and excited for the other shamans, all connecting to their hummingbirds to *make the impossible possible.*

Even though I still had visible issues around needing to be accepted by 'the elders', I had gotten used to the eye rolls and the cold shoulders. *It's not personal,* I told myself. There was a deep sense of honour in ceremony, connecting us with the mountains in Peru. At the moment my teachers passed on my lineage stone, I felt the oneness and love between us, beyond ego, beyond our shadows, beyond stories. The absolute gratitude I had for them for delivering this medicine to me flowed with my tears, and most of all, I had a huge sense of gratitude to myself for stepping up and saying yes despite all the obstacles and discomfort along the way.

The medicine of the Andes was strong in me. My soul had called me there all my life. I was exactly where I was meant to be.

My friend Simon drove me home at the end of our week. We were both full of joy and stillness. He had become a true brother to me and I was grateful for our friendship. I told him all about the herons I'd seen flying to and from the medicine wheel and that I was expecting to see as we drove home. But none came. I let it go, grateful for all the other times they had come to affirm I was on the right track.

He dropped me off at a roundabout in Slough where I could wait for Harry to come and pick me up. I stood in this concrete jungle, a million miles away from the nurture and nature I had been in. The sky was getting dark, the street lights were coming on and I was regretting not having my coat on, when a heron flew out of a tree behind me. It swept low, just over my head. I could not stop laughing. Miraculous, hilarious, brilliant.

"Thank you, thank you, thank you!" I shouted. And of course!

I got my phone out and called Simon.

"I just saw a fucking heron fly right over my head. It was so low I could have touched it!"

Simon laughed, and in his posh old English accent, he replied endearingly, "Of course you saw a heron, darling Lou. I wouldn't expect anything less."

***

Sacred call

Ten years to the day after Avalon was seeded into my belly, on the first dark moon of November, a new cosmic energy came to me, firing up my soul's purpose and awakening me to a new journey that had the potential to break all our roots. It shook my soul awake in the middle of the night and sang into my ear.

Apus Illimani hampe hampe.

The mountain spirit sang as I lay still as a log, freaked out at what was happening. I knew this song. This was the song from a shamanic class I'd been to a few weeks before. I recognised Illimani as one of the many sacred mountains in Peru, but why was it being sung in my ear in the dead of night by some highly powerful spirit energy fully alive all about me?

I pulled the duvet over my head and willed myself to go back to sleep, feeling like a child who was afraid of ghosts, not wanting to think about it too much. I didn't want to be awake any more. I wanted to get a good sleep.

The next morning, like most mornings, I woke to the safety of Harry's arms reaching out for me and pulling me closer into his body. This simple way of waking up, which happens 99% of our days, is what brings stillness to my morning. I reflected briefly from my safe haven. In truth, I knew I could fly. I had sensed everything that had gone before was mere preparation for what was to come.

The next night, I fell into bed with Harry. Our bedding was old and comfortable with pulls from the cats clawing. Our room was half-decorated and our ensuite needed finishing. Our windows had no curtains. It seemed I could manifest most of what I needed in life by the skin of my teeth, but luxury was at the bottom of our values. Yet climbing into bed, curling up next to Harry's body, warming my freezing feet, I was blessed. It's all I needed.

I woke again at that sacred hour when it was neither day nor night, when there was no sound and no light. This time, what woke me was gentle enough to not shock me and strong enough to rouse me from sleep.

Apus Illimani hampe hampe.

The same song. Round and round in my head. My mind kicked in, clocking that the song was the same as the night before. Now this was definitely weird. My heart knew Mount Illimani was calling me. I could feel its presence in my room. But I'd never had a mountain call me before and I didn't know what to do with it, so I ignored it again, rolled towards Harry and switched off.

This time, when I woke up in the morning, the first thing I did was message my shamanic teacher:

So the past two mornings I've woken to what I am assuming is Mt Illimani calling me. The name goes round and round my head from that song and I can feel it. I've never been called by a mountain before. Angels, spirits, I understand, but this I don't. Any ideas?

She replied right away:

Yes, Illimani is calling you! The mountains do call us. I guess you'll be coming to Peru with us next May!

I knew she'd say that. But how could I go to Peru without my family or any money? I messaged back:

I could never go to Peru without Harry. We have always wanted to do that together. And there is no way we could leave the kids with someone for two weeks!

She didn't drop it:

Tricky then. How old are they?

I replied:

5 and 9. I know I'm being called but I can't leave my family behind.

And she agreed the girls would be far too young, as the trip was tough emotionally. I told her I'd have to keep listening to the call. Before I got going, I went back and forth over the Peru question to see if anything came up.

I recalled Harry and me lying in bed in my old student house talking about the places we wanted to go. We'd both wanted to visit Peru, though for different reasons. He was taken by the history of it, the Nazca lines and the science behind the Inca. For me, it was purely for the music. My heart sunk as I even imagined going without him. I couldn't.

A memory I had forgotten popped up. It was of a tape I'd found in a hippy shop when I was about 13. The tape had a mountain on it and two Peruvian people with panpipes. Back then, I had yearned to hear that music on a mountaintop in real life, to be there in the music, but that tape wore as thin as my dreams of Peru. That memory was a sign and these synergies were no longer weird. I had to go to Peru, didn't I?

Remembering that tape, I realised this was what it had all been about. All my life, my soul had pointed that way. What was I going to do though? I truly couldn't bear to go without Harry and we couldn't take the kids. I also couldn't leave them. I couldn't do that to them. As for Harry, I had spent so much of the past few years constantly pushing the boundaries of our relationship that I'd looked like a crazy woman at times. This was one push too far. I couldn't entertain the idea. I carried on with my day and tried to put it aside.

That night, I wasn't woken by the mountains, but my dreams were intense. They reflected the relationship I had with my teacher. In the teaching room, I was asking her where my lineage stone was from. I wanted to know if it was from Illimani. She was cold and annoyed at my interruption. She shooed me away, telling me to look in a bag of rocks and stones, because they all had tags on. One would look like mine.

She went off to teach the group, and although I was conscious of being annoying, I persisted. I had to find out what mountain was mine. As she walked off, she paused. I sensed she had to give me something but didn't want me to have it. There was envy coming from her, but also responsibility that she had to give me whatever it was. She pulled out a big black rock with a metal piece sticking out. She almost threw it at me and couldn't bear to look back.

The rock had symbols all over it. Some even looked like Reiki symbols. I tried taking pictures on my phone because I knew it was a message I needed to remember and understand. I had to decode it. But when I looked at the screen, I couldn't see the symbols.

I woke up. Now things were serious. This dream was too powerful to ignore. I was a bit shaky and wanted music to soothe my soul for my morning meditation, but didn't know what I felt like listening to, so I threw on Spotify radio and let the Universe choose the music for me. The music was loud and powerful, and transported me away from my ego, which was currently wondering what the fuck was wrong with me. I surrendered to whatever would flow through me.

I did my shamanic breathing, but I wasn't loving it. In fact, I was annoyed at it. Everything was annoying me, so I opened my mesa. I'd never opened my mesa for meditation before, but I was all over the place and looking for anything to anchor me.

Then the mountains called again. Over the sound of the music playing, Illimani sang its loud, relentless call.

Apus Illimani hampe hampe.

I was fearful, confused and not fully in my own body. I knew change was on the horizon and that it wasn't going to be easy. I sobbed into my medicine mesa that now held 10 kuyas — medicine stones. I picked up my beautiful heart-shaped medicine stone, my very first one, and instinctively called in my serpent. I began speaking though her, as if I was her, as if I was speaking to God.

You can't ask me to come to go to Peru! You can't ask me!

Then something happened that shook me to my core... The mountain replied.

WHY?

Out of my body, I was shaking and reached for another kuya. I called in my jaguar but I was lost. I picked up another medicine stone on autopilot, without knowing which it was. I cried and sobbed and crumpled on the floor over my mesa. I dug deep to release all that was stopping me.

It's too big. You can't ask me to leave my family.

I cried. The words I was sending up were almost primal, raw. My belly hurt, as fear gripped me. The mountain replied again.

WHY?

It was beyond all reality. But it was reality. Me here, shaking on the floor, searching inside for the reason I couldn't leave my family and go to Peru.

And then I saw all my fears: Harry working in the office just off the kitchen, stressed about paying the tax bill and the mortgage; the kids running around the kitchen and him feeling more pressure because he couldn't get anything done. And me? I was absent. I wasn't there.

I sobbed my last sob and replied to the mountain, this time with surrender, exhausted.

Because it will make Harry sad.

The mountain spoke again.

What if that is an assumption?

I lifted my head from my ego death. The fear in my heart dropped into my belly where it was transformed into knowing. I knew I was going to Peru on my own and I knew there was no other option.

I relaxed my shoulders and told the mountain with surrender and new strength, "I will come to Peru, but you need to send me the money, a lot of money. This has to be big. Enough for me to come to Peru and more. So big that Harry will believe and trust in my calling and ability to manifest. Enough that he will never doubt me."

A song came on that I'd never heard before. I cried and laughed at the same time to the sounds of *Song Of Your Heart* by Peter Kater and Snatam Kaur. I breathed and closed my mesa. This work was done.

Then I realised what day it was: November 2nd. My nan's 85th birthday was the next day.

I knew too well the power of manifesting and I knew too well my own power. I didn't want anything to happen to her. I didn't want this money to be an inheritance. I had to be more specific. Panicking, I reopened my mesa and picked up a stone, as though it was a telephone line direct to the mountain spirit.

"This money isn't to come from an inheritance. This has to come from somewhere it isn't missed. It has to be clean. It has to be win-win."

I packed up my mesa, feeling more in control. I didn't have to do anything that wasn't on my terms. I was free of my fears and worries. I detached from the outcome and got on with my day.

***

I looked out the window late that evening. There was snow outside. Gaia was calling. *Come, come. Come outside.* I knew that call. And I knew to go when I was called. So I wrapped up, coat and boots always by the back door these days, ready to go outside when I heard it. The ice crunched underneath my feet as I walked to the top of the garden. It was coming along nicely now. So much had changed in a year, in two years, in four.

I'm clambered up the slope, clumsy and looking ridiculous, but I enjoyed the challenge of the elements these days and seemed to have manifested a miniature mountain of my own, even if it was a 20-foot mound at the back of our house. On top sat an antique garden fawn figure, brought to me by one of our builders who had an angelic experience with me and said I saved his life.

Scrambling uphill, I focused on getting to the cherry tree. I felt different. Everything felt different, clearer. I held the tree, shivering on the outside, but warm from peace and comfort of being with this old friend. I took a breath and looked out to the world, one hand holding the tree, the other holding my stomach. And then that feeling washed through me.

Paralysis in bliss.

I began to shake, tremors in my body, but such beauty. I wasn't in control and when I closed my eyes, everything was white on the inside. I could breathe, but that was about all.

I could have stayed there all day if I chose, but I didn't even have that choice. Something was happening. I was downloading. My head filled with light and my feet pulled light up from the earth, like coming up on drugs: rushing, love, bliss. *Oh my God, this is beyond anything. Like an* orgasm. *I'm being activated, shaking, I'm trembling. I'm being filled with light. Am I dying? I'm in heaven.*

I began to feel my body coming back into the world. Everything was brighter. I knew this feeling. I'd felt it years ago sitting on the doorstep after being attacked. And when I'd first gone to Glastonbury and everything had been beautiful — so fucking beautiful. *I have to write about this.*

I took the message and acted straight away. This was it. The tree had given me the goddess energy. I had formed into the tree goddess leading the way to consciousness. I wrote.

I am here to protect the trees, the earth. I am here to bring the next generation home. I'm gonna do this in the most magical way.

***

The next morning, I sat in the Room of Requirement, surrounded by all I had manifested, even down to the wallpaper, the handmade shelves, the chair I was sitting on. I loved this room and was enjoying being still, when Harry shouted through.

"There's a letter for you, babe."

"Is it brown?" I joked.

"No, it looks interesting. Come open it."

Normally, we picked up the mail and shoved it on the side to be ignored for months on end. The fact he was telling me I had some 'interesting' mail raised fears in me. Yet I was so connected right now that no letter was going to move me from this place of stillness. It took three times for him to call me into the kitchen before I rose from my meditative state. On the kitchen counter was a large white square envelope. It looked bigger than a card, but our address was handwritten, so I assumed it was a wedding invite. I racked my brains to think who was getting married this coming year, as I picked it up and tore it open. As I did, I noticed tiny gold writing on the front of the envelope saying 'you're one in a million.' It was from a former student.

I opened the card and held a two-page letter in one hand and... something else in the other. Something un-fucking-believable.

A cheque for £25,000. I fell to my knees.

"I can't take this. I need to give it back to her."

Crying and shaking, all I could see was Harry looking down at me on the floor and the cheque in my hands. Through the sobs, I wailed, "The mountains called me. They woke me in my sleep. They have been calling me to go to Peru. Yesterday I told them if they wanted me to go, they had to send me the money and it had to be big. Enough that you would trust in me and my calling."

Time stood still. I tried reading the letter, but I couldn't see it. My head was in a thousand places. Eventually, I could see well enough. As I spoke the words aloud, I tried to process it, but it didn't really sink in. Not Harry though. He heard it. And it changed everything in him...

The letter thanked me for helping this woman in her darkest days. Without my love and support, she said, she wouldn't have made it through a huge legal case she'd been enduring. To me, this was nothing. It was easy to help people. It didn't take any thought. And it was always unconditional. I just listened to the call and answered it. I never expected anything in return. It was just what I did. This was too much...

But the letter explained how this gift of money couldn't come close to how much she valued what I did for her and so many others in the world. My heart was being forced open to receive acknowledgement for my work, a moment of seeing what I did for people.

Then the words that were to seal the magic jumped from the second page. She explained how six months earlier the angels had whispered an amount to send me that would enable me to make important journeys.

Important journeys. I stared at the words. This was incredible!

She signed off with love, saying she was excited for what lay ahead for me and my family.

I was in shock. My soul knew what this miracle was, but my mind could not fathom the manifestation and divine timing of what was happening. There was no denying now that there was a greater plan for me.

Harry looked down and smiled.

"Lou, you have to go to Peru," he said proudly. "And buy me a car," he joked.

I laughed, then watched his demeanour change. He paced the kitchen, shaking his head, in shock.

He turned back to me, "You deserve this, Lou. You've worked hard and you're always there for everyone. I'm just so proud of you."

I smiled at him, soaking in his soft, humbled energy. For the first time in forever, I was lost for words.

Harry continued pacing, then added, "I don't know what I know anymore. But I know I don't know."

***

The air glowed gold around me and I knew. I knew everything was going to be alright. I had never felt so safe, so held, so devoted. I had never felt such trust in the Universe as I did in this moment. I could die right this second, leave everything and everyone behind, and know they were safe.

Nothing made sense, but nothing needed to anymore, because my heart and soul knew it all. I had sailed here alone, through rough seas of emotion. I had fallen overboard and climbed back on. I had steered my boat through strange seas, sometimes with no crew to help me. And I'd wondered if I was ever going to find my way home.

I didn't even know where home was, but I'd made it. I'd made it to a land that was only real in my heart and mind, a place I'd been ridiculed for believing was real. But I'd always felt there was something more.

In this moment of bliss and elation, I knew I would never question myself again. I would never doubt what my heart told me, because I trusted it. I knew my heart was pure and guided me down a path of integrity. This is what led me to the greatest places.

For the first time in my life, I had created something physical to show to the world, to show my husband, that what I spoke of was real. What was happening to me on the inside was now visible to the world. A miracle had happened.

Now there was no fighting, no need to prove my calling to the mystical lands, no feelings of judgment, no-one rolling their eyes, no laughing me off my course. I had landed. Suddenly, they were looking at me with pride.

With Harry, that was all I had ever wanted — his blessing and acceptance — because I couldn't do it without him. And now he was saying I deserved this, telling me he was so proud. After all these years, I was free to walk a life of purpose. I had a calling. And even though this meant I would be alone at times, his love and support were like the sun and moon coming together and colluding to keep the earth turning. Our roots went so deep that I could sense the pure trust.

I gazed up at the wall as I sipped my tea and my eyes were drawn to the far-right corner of the vision board I'd made at Mary's workshop. In disbelief, I laughed out loud as the board revealed another layer.

"Of fucking course!" I said aloud to no-one in particular.

There, over a lush green picture of Amazon rainforest, were the words "Welcome to the Jungle!" that I had not comprehended at the time I chose them. In the centre of the board was a strong woman, completely naked yet fully in her power, picking up a telephone.

"Answering a call," I murmured. *She is me.*

This trip to Peru would involve five nights in the Amazon jungle. It was as if the Universe already knew. Was this the plan all along? Peru had called me since I was 13 years old. I was about to answer that call and learn what the mountains really required of me.

***

MY DEEPEST THANKS...

TO HARRY, THANK YOU for your unconditional love and support, for the passion, laughter and commitment you make to a life of fearless growth, wonder and divine union with me.

To Bon Bon and Bellaboo, thank you for your pure open-hearted love of life. You are my greatest teachers. Your dancing, giggles, kisses and cuddles are pure medicine. I am in awe of your unwavering courage to always be true to yourselves. May your unconditional love for each other and the world inspire light on the earth.

To my family, thank you for my life, for raising me. Mom, for leading by example in being a pillar for our families and communities. Dad, for teaching me that music is the greatest connector and the silent language of love. My stepdad, for embedding a positive mental attitude in me since I was a little girl. My nan and late grandad, for being a comfort to my soul when I was learning to be on this earth.

To my soul family, some of you are in this book, most of you are not, yet you still play the most incredible part in my life. There are not enough words to say thank you for the journeys we have taken. I love you so much.

To Kris, my editor, I knew I was going to work with you when the universe gave me your name all those years ago.

We have been on such a journey. Thank you for seeing me and holding me through this immense journey of heart opening, soul shaking and terrifying revealing of myself!

And to the friends who walked with me in the last days of editing, thank you, thank you, thank you. Your encouragement, time, support and commitment to helping was invaluable.

Finally, to my community and students... You rock! Your support is mind-blowing. Wow! This book is for you guys. *Yes!*

Thank you to my teachers past and present. The lessons and relationships were bright and sometimes painful, but I honour and thank you for the roles you played. I love you and honour the gifts you have given me to stand in my power and show up no matter what.

I give thanks with the deepest of reverence for the guidance of the divine beings that love me unconditionally. I am at your service.

***

ABOUT LOUISE

LOUISE CARRON HARRIS IS a modern-day medicine woman; a shaman, healer, teacher, storyteller, radio presenter, and public speaker. She lives in the southeast of England with her husband and children.

She lives a life of love, laugher, and contentment, while inspiring others through powerful experiences, classes and retreats.

You can contact Louise on: hello@louisecarronharris.com
and follow her on social media:
    www.facebook.com/louisecarronharris
    Instagram @louisecarronharris
    Twitter @loucarronharris

***

Printed in Great Britain
by Amazon